SOUTHBRIDGE

Part Two
of
The City of the Bayou
Collection

Reginald Edmund

BROADWAY PLAY PUBLISHING INC
New York
BroadwayPlayPub.com

SOUTHBRIDGE
© Copyright 2021 Reginald Edmund

Cover image by Daniel Winters

First edition: June 2021
I S B N: 978-0-88145-866-4

Book design: Marie Donovan
Page make-up: Adobe InDesign
Typeface: Palatino

In memory of
Russ Tutterow
(1946-2015)

The City of the Bayou Collection is a series of nine plays. They are the playwright's attempt at making a contemporary House of Atreus through a Afro-Surrealist lens. The plays, in order, are:

THE DAUGHTERS OF THE MOON

SOUTHBRIDGE

IN THE PROPHET'S HOUSE

BLOOD ON THE BAYOU

REDEMPTION OF ALLAH BLACK

JUNETEENTH STREET

THE ORDAINED SMILE OF SAINT SADIE MAY JENKINS

THE LAST CADILLAC

ALL THE DYING VOICES

Christopher C Davis (Stranger), the protagonist of this play is the son of Kokuma, the protagonist of THE DAUGHTERS OF THE MOON.

SOUTHBRIDGE was a 2009 National Runner-Up for the Lorraine Hansberry and the Rosa Parks Playwriting Awards at the Kennedy Center American College Theater Festival, the 2010 winner of the Southern Playwrights Competition, and 2013 Winner of the Lorraine Hansberry Award at the Black Theater Alliance Awards.

SOUTHBRIDGE was originally produced as a
Graduate School Thesis at the 2009 Seabury Quinn Jr
Playwrights' Festival—Ohio University Theatre in,
May 2009. The cast and creative contributors were:

CHRISTOPHER C DAVIS (STRANGER)......... Tyler Rollinson
NADIA DAVIS...Clara Jackson
LUCINDA LUCKEY..Georgia Guy
EDWIN BERRY..Eric Lynch
SHERIFF WARDEN .... Adam Meredith

Director..Vanessa Mercado Taylor
Set design.. Evan K Schmidt
Associate set design .... Cassandra Westover
Lighting design......................................Adam N Suntken
Costume designer.. Jenifer Redman
Associate costume design..............................Celia Childress
Sound design..Cassie Devine
Stage designer ....Jennifer Sachs
Dramaturgy ....Casey Clem & Nicole Simon

SOUTHBRIDGE received its world premiere at Chicago Dramatists Theatre (Russ Tutterow, Artistic Director) in March 2013. The cast and creative contributors were:

CHRISTOPHER C DAVIS (STRANGER) .... Manny Buckley
NADIA DAVIS .... Ashley Honore Roberson
LUCINDA LUCKEY .... Wendy Robie
EDWIN BERRY .... Lance Newton
SHERIFF WARDEN .... Gene Cordon

Director .... Russ Tutterow
Set design .... Michael Mroch
Lighting design .... Jeff Pines
Sound design .... Joseph Fosco
Costume design .... Samantha C Jones
Fight choreographer .... Chris Rickett
Stage manager .... Jennifer J Thusing

CHARACTERS & SETTING

CHRISTOPHER C DAVIS (STRANGER), *Black male, 23 years old*

NADIA DAVIS, *Black female, mid 20s*

EDWIN C BERRY, *Black male, 30s*

LUCINDA LUCKEY, *White female, mid 50s*

SHERIFF TIMOTHY WARD, *White male, early 50s*

The Fall Months of 1881
The Township of Athens, Ohio

Note: The stage is to be set with a tree stump in the center stage, large tangles of rope wrapped around it. Crescent behind the stump is to be four plain rough hewed wood benches. In front on two opposite side of the stump there are two benches of similar design. Ideally, the play should be fluid, allowing the scenes to be woven together and collide into each other. This play although fictionalized was inspired by the Athens, Ohio lynching of 1881.

ADDITIONAL NOTES:

Deliberate space within dialogue is means for hard pauses.

(…) A breath between words not a pause or a trailing off

(—) Indicates the speaker is cut off mid sentence

Prologue

(A singular red light pierces through the darkness of the stage revealing a black man named CHRISTOPHER *standing atop a tree stump. Indistinct whispers)*

(He stands half naked arms outstretched. He hums a mournful pain filled song softly to himself, as if in heartbroken mourning.)

CHRISTOPHER: Do you know what it means to truly love?
Love so much that it'll swallow you whole.
Choke you till you can't breathe.
I don't think you do.
I know I didn't until I learned what it meant…

*(*CHRISTOPHER *begins humming the same haunting tune again as the lights dim swallowing him into the darkness.)*

(Black out)

ACT ONE
Book of Recollection

(In the lonely darkness, angry voices can be heard. A jail cell, two figures stand opposite each other, there is a feeling of cold distance and isolation CHRISTOPHER *paces back and forth singing nervously,* SHERIFF WARD *enters unnoticed.)*

CHRISTOPHER: *(Singing)*
Somewhere in the garden of Eden…
A tree stands twisted…
Somewhere in the garden of Eden…
A tree stands twisted…
A tree stands twisted…

*(*WARD *applauds* CHRISTOPHER *mockingly.)*

WARD: Bravo, boy, Bravo.

CHRISTOPHER: What's going on outside?
What's all that noise out there?
You got to atleast tell me what I'm even in here for?
I ain't even done nothing!

WARD: It's cold as hell outside…
Think this might be the worst November storm we'll ever get yet.
Stop pacing and calm down… Why don't you have a seat for me?

CHRISTOPHER: What you arrest me for?

WARD: Sit down—

CHRISTOPHER: You had no cause to arrest me.

WARD:Will you sit damnit?!!

(CHRISTOPHER *sits.*)

WARD:Thank you.
You thirsty?
Coffee, milk perhaps?
I'd offer you some of this.
(He pulls out a flask.)
But you don't drink do you?

CHRISTOPHER: Just tell me what's all that commotion out there about?

WARD: It's about you.

CHRISTOPHER: I haven't done nothing.

WARD: Mind if I sit?
(He sits.)
Nice waistcoat, where'd you get it?

(Silence)

(CHRISTOPHER *takes off the waistcoat.*)

WARD:Can you hear that?
That is the sound of a mob gathering.
You got the town folks here all sorts of worked up.
You are in serious trouble, Christopher…
You should have taken my offer,
None of this would be happening if you did.
That mob is going to be banging on this door soon.
They want to string you up.
And I've been told I'm expected to hand you over.

CHRISTOPHER: This ain't right…
I didn't do anything.
I know me and you, haven't always seen eye to eye,
But I don't even know what I'm doing here, Sheriff.

WARD: Where to start?
Christopher Davis, Twenty two years of age…
(He whistles.)
Bail for freedom set at three hundred dollars…
Arrested and imprisoned for committing violence and
outrage upon the person of Lucinda Luckey—

CHRISTOPHER: Widow Luckey?!! I didn't attack that
woman.
I wouldn't do that.

WARD: You know, it's a miracle she's alive.
Now listen to me and listen to me real good.
I don't want to see you hanging from some tree,
If you're innocent, I want to help you.
In my opinion, mob justice ain't no justice at all.
I just want what's right, what's right and proper.

(CHRISTOPHER looks at WARD for a long time.)

WARD: What?
Why you lookin' at me like that?

CHRISTOPHER: Just see you for who you really are, sir.

WARD: I want you to convince me of your innocence
or…
Confess that you attacked Widow Luckey.
Now I'm not certain you did it,
But if you're guilty I want you to take this paper.
(He takes out a sheet of paper.)
…And put your name next to it and say you did the
crime.
I want you to do the right thing.

(There's a moment CHRISTOPHER looks towards WARD.)

CHRISTOPHER: I wouldn't hurt a soul, sheriff.

WARD: I just want to know what happened.

CHRISTOPHER: Somehow I don't believe you.

WARD: It's simple, Christopher… real simple…
It's an election year, boy…
I don't want anything to dirty my name,
Your death on my watch is…
Well, It doesn't serve my interests.

(EDWIN BERRY appears.)

EDWIN: Yes my friend, the time to strike is now.

WARD: That mob outside gave me an hour.

EDWIN: Alright, remember what I told you, now.

WARD: So how about you start talkin'…

(CHRISTOPHER cross to EDWIN.)

EDWIN: Allow me to do all the talkin', alright?
I happen to have a gift when it comes to dealin' with
her type.

CHRISTOPHER: Her type?

EDWIN: Yes, white people—

CHRISTOPHER: White people?—

EDWIN: I got an understandin' of them,
The way they think…
I speak Caucasian,
It's like French…or Yiddish,
It's like a second language to me.

CHRISTOPHER: I think that's the most ridiculous thing,
I've ever heard you tell me.

EDWIN: Now I know it might sound hard to believe,
However you have your gift, and I got mine…
So pay attention now, you might learn something.
Stand up straight, and look presentable—

CHRISTOPHER: What if this doesn't work?

EDWIN: Oh, I'm going to get that signature…

I'm going to get that signature one way or the other...
Remember stick to the plan...
You work for that lady, you get close to that lady...
You gain that lady's trust,
Use some of your charm to talk up the hotel a bit,
Then when the time is right,
You allow me to slide in and have her sign the loan.
Tread gently though, Since her husband died,
She's become a rather mean spirited woman...
Tenacious with her questionings...
Got a bite worst than any dog I've ever encountered—

CHRISTOPHER: I still don't see why I have to be the one to do this.

EDWIN: She's not exactly partial to my company...

LUCINDA: Oh, what a pleasant surprise.
Morning, Edwin, may I help you?
Edwin mannerism in posture and speaking becomes heighten

EDWIN: Oh, what a pleasant morning it is, isn't it, Mrs Luckey?

LUCINDA: It is... How's that pretty wife of yours?

EDWIN: Martha, oh, she's at a luncheon at Wilberforce—

CHRISTOPHER: Good mornin' to you, ma'am.

LUCINDA: Mornin'.

EDWIN: I recalled that you had come by my restaurant,
Just a few days ago saying you were in need of some assistance, to tend your land.
Well, recently my dear good friend here, Mr Davis,
Found himself in the need of employment.
Me being the good Christian that I am, as you know...

I decided I should perhaps come by and introduce you
two,
In hopes that you might be able to arrange,
A suitable business transaction favorable to both ya'll
needs.

LUCINDA: I see—

CHRISTOPHER: You do need someone to work your land
don't you, ma'am?

LUCINDA: You have experience?

EDWIN: Oh, he has plenty of experience.
A plethora of experiences to say the least.
This man right here has plenty of admirable traits,
Certainly a man of highest character.

LUCINDA: Well, Edwin, you're known in this valley,
for…
How shall I put it, being the slickest snake in the
garden.
However, I'm certain the young man can speak for
himself.

CHRISTOPHER: I got enough.

LUCINDA: How old are you?

CHRISTOPHER: I'm twenty two, about to be twenty
three, ma'am-.

LUCINDA: You're nothin' but a babe—

CHRISTOPHER: I got good hands, and a strong back…
I'm just asking for work.

(LUCINDA *smiles.*)

LUCINDA: I'll pay ten dollars for a good month's worth
of labor.

CHRISTOPHER: Missus, you make it twelve and fifty
cents.

EDWIN / LUCINDA: What?

CHRISTOPHER: Twelve fifty, you got yourself a deal.

(LUCINDA *studies* CHRISTOPHER.)

LUCINDA: That's steep.

CHRISTOPHER: I'm looking at your property…
No offense, ma'am, but…
You need more than just that field worked.

LUCINDA: I'm not going any higher than ten fifty.

CHRISTOPHER: For twelve even…I'll fix that door of yours,
It shouldn't be off its hinges like that…
I'm only going that low cause you look like a good, kind woman.

LUCINDA: Why do you say that?

CHRISTOPHER: Eyes don't lie to me, never have.
So what you say?

EDWIN: Excuse me, Mrs Luckey,
I need to speak with this young gentlemen for a moment.

LUCINDA: Of course.

EDWIN: (*To* CHRISTOPHER) God gave you common sense, boy, where is it?
You can't talk to no white woman that way,
This woman just offered you ten fifty,
That's more money than you'd see down in the coal mines,
Laying bricks, or any other job you can put your hands on.
Christopher, be reasonable and work with this woman.

CHRISTOPHER: That's exactly what we're doing,
Edwin…
(*To* LUCINDA)

Well, do we have ourselves a deal ma'am?

LUCINDA: Who do you think I am a Rockefeller?
I'm not going any higher than eleven dollars.

CHRISTOPHER: Now ma'am…
A minute ago you said you weren't going any higher
than ten fifty…
Looks like you need shingles to that roof up there fix
too…I'll fix whatever else needs fixin'.
Eleven fifty, ma'am, And I'm all yours.

LUCINDA: Best be careful, Edwin, you've got trouble
here.

EDWIN: Believe me I know.

LUCINDA: *(To* CHRISTOPHER*)* Young man, maybe you
forgot, but you came to me for work—

EDWIN: That is quite a brilliant observation,
Perhaps you should put that into consideration.

CHRISTOPHER: I am, Mr Berry.
Now you're right, Mrs Luckey…
I did knock on your door…
But lookin' at all the work you need done over here…
I could go elsewhere. It's your choice.

LUCINDA: What's your name again?

EDWIN: It's Christopher Davis—

CHRISTOPHER: She asked me, Edwin…
Everybody call me Stranger though.

(Silence)

LUCINDA: You say you're name is Stranger?

CHRISTOPHER: Yes ma'am.

LUCINDA: I see.
(Pause)
Some people say that you signed your soul to the devil,

and he left his mark on you, that true?

CHRISTOPHER: What else you hear?

LUCINDA: That everyone you come near meets tragedy.
That you see things…visions.
There's talk I hear that you're responsible for that baby
dying like it did.
Put a conjure on it—

CHRISTOPHER: Now that's one lie that can stop right
here!—

EDWIN: She's just tellin' you what she's heard.

CHRISTOPHER: You believe everything you hear?

LUCINDA: Well, No—

CHRISTOPHER: Let's get something clear, I ain't sold
away my soul to nobody…
First and foremost,I believe in God, Miss Luckey,
Now whether he sees me or not is another story.
Second, I wouldn't hurt a soul, ma'am
And thirdly—

EDWIN: Third… It's just third—

CHRISTOPHER: Thank you, and third, as far as what
people around here, Wishes and chooses to say about
me…
I let people say what they want to say.
And believe what they want to believe.
Now, that being said, what do you believe?

LUCINDA: I prefer to find out for myself.
I got that choice don't I?

CHRISTOPHER: You do indeed, ma'am.

(CHRISTOPHER *looks at* LUCINDA. *She looks at him.*)

(*Silence*)

LUCINDA: Why'd you look at me like that?

CHRISTOPHER: I'm sorry ma'am, meant no harm by it.

LUCINDA: Well, no doubt, I'm certain people mention me as well.

CHRISTOPHER: Just like you, I prefer to find out for myself.
So do I got myself a job, ma'am?

LUCINDA: Well then that depends, Stranger.
First don't call me ma'am, makes me feel old.

CHRISTOPHER: And second?

LUCINDA: On whether, you're going to take eleven dollars even.
Your choice… So what's it going to be, Stranger?

(CHRISTOPHER *crosses left to jail cell.*)

CHRISTOPHER: Look just because Lucinda, said my name—

WARD: Lucinda?

CHRISTOPHER: Just because Widow Luckey, said my name,
That doesn't give you evidence to arrest me on.
I'm telling you, I ain't done anything.

(WARD *shows* CHRISTOPHER *a hatchet and places it on the ground in front of him.*)

WARD: You've been accused of breaking into her house at midnight with this right here—

CHRISTOPHER: Where'd you get that?—

WARD: So it's yours, I take it?

CHRISTOPHER: I ain't sayin' that.

(WARD *places hatchet on table down left.*)

WARD: From what we've gathered,
You beat her, strangled her to the floor,
And had your way with her…

Then you took this here hatchet, and struck her.
Struck her without mercy, over and over again—

(Lights up on NADIA *busy at work in the kitchen a basket is in her hand. She's humming softly to herself as she places items into it.)*

CHRISTOPHER: I wouldn't do that.

WARD: So this hatchet, don't belong to you?
(Silence)
Answer me...
(To CHRISTOPHER'*s house.)*
I'm going to ask you one more time...
Yes or no, Miss Nadia,
have you seen your husband today?

NADIA: Sir, when are you going to start callin' me by my married name?
Cause it's been three months now, Sheriff,
So I'm just curious?

WARD: Yes...or no?

NADIA: Let's start by you saying "Good afternoon, Nadia."
That would be the polite way to come over and question me.

WARD: Good Afternoon, Nadia.

NADIA: Afternoon Sheriff, isn't it a lovely day?
Now what could bring you around to bless my presence?

WARD: Child, Quit with the theatrics,
Just answer my question, will you?
Is that husband of yours around?

NADIA: He's off with Mr Berry somewhere, sir.

WARD: Berry, huh?

NADIA: Yes sir.

WARD: I don't trust that man as far as I can throw him.

NADIA: Yes, sir.

WARD: You hear what your husband did to the Jenkin's newborn?

NADIA: My husband keeps no secrets from me.

WARD: Really?

(Pause)

NADIA: Yes sir.

WARD: I'm curious, did He tell you he walked up to the Jenkin's door, Knocked and as Mrs Jenkin goes and answers it,
Supposedly he put his hands on her and curse that baby—

NADIA: I'm sure that He was only trying to help.

WARD: Help huh?
Seems to me he destroys everything he touches.
Wonder if you knew this…
Three days after he went over there, that baby born dead,
Umbilical wrapped around its throat.
This morning to be exact.
(Pause)
He didn't tell you that, did he?
(Silence)

NADIA: I'm sorry to hear that.

WARD: Tell that to the Jenkin's family.
They're raising up a storm talkin' about conjures being put on them…
I don't need this kind of mess in my town, you hear me?

NADIA: Clear as Jaysus when he did the sermon on the mount.

WARD: Now, Nadia, I'm gonna need you to do me a favor.
I'm hearing he's walkin' around with a hatchet in his belt.

NADIA: I don't know nothing about some hatchet.

WARD: That little brawl outside the Putnam's,
Now these curses among other things.
That boy got folks around town nervous.
That's the last thing I need to add to my headache about him,
Along side that "let me look into your eyes" mess,
People gonna start to think, He's out to cause trouble.

NADIA: I'm curious, Sheriff?
The town folks thinkin', he's out to cause trouble,
Cause he can see things others can't?
Cause he's supposedly carrying around a hatchet?
Or is it simply cause he's a colored?

WARD: This is a progressive town.

NADIA: Is that why the McHenrys, and the Winfields, and the Harrisons are all talkin' about movin' away?
Is that why coloreds are scared to walk the streets at night? Progressive town? Tell that to poor Lil' Sammy Boy.
His folks found him with his eye knocked out behind the train depot.
You punish those wealthy college gents who did it?
Did you even look for them, sheriff?

WARD: I'm just tellin' you, purely out of genuine concern for you.

NADIA: I'm a grown woman, sheriff.

WARD: Nadia.

(Silence)

I'm concerned about you, child.

I have the right to be concerned.

That's all. How long have I known you, huh?

Known you since you were about knee high,

So small I could hold you in one hand. Remember?

NADIA: I remember, sir.

WARD: Didn't I always come by and I treat you and
your momma good?

Check up on you every now and then?

Make sure nobody came around and bother you and
your family?

When you had nothing in that house, who fed you,
child?

Who did your mother come to so she could pay for you
to get proper schooling, only to watch you squander it?

Didn't I do all those things or did you forget?

(There is a slight uneasy pause.)

NADIA: I remember. I remember, sir.

WARD: Good.

(Pause)

Just like then, I'm simply looking out for you.

NADIA: Well I appreciate it, Sheriff.

WARD: I'm serious…

You come from a good family, child.

A good decent Christian family, and sometime…

Honestly, Nadia, I don't know what you see in that
man.

I see it clear as day,

That boy, you married to is headed for destruction,

I just don't want to see you tangled in it with him.

And I don't need no special gift of sight to see that.

NADIA: Sheriff…Strangers, is a good man…a kind man.
He's just misunderstood is all and…
I don't like you comin' over to my house,
Talkin' bad about my husband, sir.

(WARD *moves towards* NADIA. *Takes her hand into his)*

WARD: Look at you.
I forget how much you remind me of your mother.

(NADIA *removes* WARD's *hand from hers.)*

NADIA: My mother is dead, sheriff.

(Silence)

WARD: Yes…I know.
You tell that husband of yours, I'm watching him close.
(Pause)
Has he been treating you decent?

NADIA: He's fine.

WARD: Are you doing alright over here?
You got plenty of food and all, right?

NADIA: I'm fine.

WARD: Need any money to hold you over, for the time being?

NADIA: We're fine.

WARD: Well if you need anything at all don't hesitate to ask.

NADIA: Well like I said I appreciate your concern.

(WARD *turns to leave.)*

NADIA: Before you get going would you care for a drink?
It's a long way back into town.

WARD: Well, that's kind of you, thank you, but I'm just fine…

(He taps his pocket revealing a flask.)

NADIA: Sheriff.

WARD: Yeah

NADIA: I meant coffee.

WARD: No, no, no… I'm just fine, thank you.

(WARD exits…CHRISTOPHER enters…)

(He stands watching NADIA at work in the kitchen.)

NADIA: *(Singing)*
Amazing grace…
How sweet the sound
That saved a wretch like me.
I once was lost, but now I'm found.
Was blind but now I see—

CHRISTOPHER: From where I'm standin'… You lookin'
so good,
I can't tell if you're a blessin' or a curse.

NADIA: How long you been standin' there?

CHRISTOPHER: Long enough for me to work up a thirst
lookin' at you.

(CHRISTOPHER and NADIA kiss.)

NADIA: You just missed Sheriff Ward.

CHRISTOPHER: I know I saw him…Waited till he left to
come inside.

NADIA: You got to start being more careful…
You're going to get this whole town scared of you.

CHRISTOPHER: I'm not worried about a bunch of damn
hill-billy farmers.
Certainly not concerned about that high-reaching
drunk.
Thinks he's the Moral Compass of the entire Ohio
Valley.

Only thing his compass points him to is liquor.

NADIA: Watch your mouth now, Sheriff's a good man—

CHRISTOPHER: Honestly, Nadia, I don't know what you see in that man.
What that man got over you?

(Silence)

NADIA: Nothing.

CHRISTOPHER: Nothing?

NADIA: Nothing, worth talkin' about.
(She notices the hatchet.)
Get that thing out my kitchen…
You know my rules bout leavin' your tools hangin' about.

CHRISTOPHER: Yes ma'am.

NADIA: You, mind tellin' me, what happened over at the Jenkins'?

CHRISTOPHER: I'd rather, act like it never happened.

NADIA: You got to look towards it and grow from it…
So let's talk.

CHRISTOPHER: You know I had that vision three nights ago,
Next day…I went over there touched her,
Felt the baby kickin' with life inside…
And I told her to tell that baby to breathe.
I saw that child's death, Nadia.
I tried to help…I tried to warn them…
What good is this sight,
I'm cursed with if I can't help nobody?—

NADIA: Maybe that vision was meant for you to hold to yourself.
Not everybody understand you like I do.

CHRISTOPHER: I don't want to hear that mess—

(NADIA *smacks* CHRISTOPHER *on the back of the head.*)

CHRISTOPHER: Woman?!!

NADIA: Boy, I'm your wife, I have the right to be
concerned.
You were talkin' in your sleep again last night.
Still having those dreams?

CHRISTOPHER: Nothin' I can't handle…
In the mean time, you beautiful married woman, come
here…

NADIA: The roof startin' to leak again,
and the wood still needs to be cut before winter.

CHRISTOPHER: Consider me already on it… Come here.

NADIA: You know, changing the subject, don't change
things none.

CHRISTOPHER: Ain't nobody changing subjects, Come
here woman.

NADIA: Down boy, I don't got the time to be messin'
with you,
Got to go down and work Miss Carol's house—

CHRISTOPHER: You're always workin'—

NADIA: Cause you ain't.

CHRISTOPHER: Oh, you're going to be changing that
tune soon.

NADIA: I made dinner.

CHRISTOPHER: Beans and rice?

NADIA: Rice and beans.

CHRISTOPHER: One day, love, we're going to eat meat…
Stuff ourselves with it—

NADIA: Well, until you put that on the table… It's rice and beans.

I got some coffee on the stove. You want a cup?

CHRISTOPHER: I think I want a different kind of coffee…
I think I want to drink you in.

Hold one of those precious cups of yours in my hand—

NADIA: You are trouble, Stranger—

CHRISTOPHER: Yes, ma'am… I want to take a long deep drink of you.

NADIA: You're in a good mood—

CHRISTOPHER: Savor the taste of your smooth skin against my lips.

NADIA: Christopher Davis, boy, you better stop that. What's come over you—

CHRISTOPHER: If you come over here, it'll be you…
I want a lil' something to quench my thirst—

NADIA: You better stop it.
I'll scream…I swear it—

CHRISTOPHER: Good, that's exactly what I want to make you do—

NADIA: Oh, you're too much trouble…
I ain't comin', nowhere near you…
Not till you tell me what got you all excited.
Besides I haven't been feeling quite right lately.

CHRISTOPHER: What's wrong?
Need to see Doc Sutherland?

NADIA: You know we can't afford to see that man.
It'll pass… Tired that's all.
Come on now, sit down tell my about you and your day.

CHRISTOPHER: Alright then…We celebrating!

NADIA: Celebrating? What we celebrating?

CHRISTOPHER: How does eleven dollars sound to you?

NADIA: A month?

CHRISTOPHER: Better believe it, baby—

NADIA: My baby got himself a job—

CHRISTOPHER: Sure, did… sure did…
You remember Widow Luckey, cross the bridge?

NADIA: A position working under that woman could be good for us—

CHRISTOPHER: Edwin Berry and I went over there earlier this morning…

(Silence)

NADIA: You workin' this job to put food on this table? Or you trying to get in on that silly dream?

CHRISTOPHER: Nadia, not again—

NADIA: The foolishness that man put in your head about a hotel…

CHRISTOPHER: He's my friend…only friend I got—

NADIA: Jaysus said the same thing about Judas.
What Edwin did to Mr Lewis restaurant was shameful.
He's a weed… He chokes out anything that tries to grow in this town that doesn't have his hand on it.
You need to cut him loose… I tell you that much.
Taste of ambition made him a selfish man.

CHRISTOPHER: Ain't nuthin' wrong with a man wantin' a lil' more…
Edwin owns an ice cream shop, a restaurant, and he's on the board over at Wilberforce,
People around him see him.
If that makes him a weed, then that's what I want?
Look at my momma, she wanted more…

Don't make her a weed, now does it?
Woman ran-away to the Ohio Valley for freedom.—

NADIA: Christopher, It's not even a colored hotel.—

CHRISTOPHER: Let me have my dreams, Nadia, that's all
I'm asking.
Don't see me tellin' you, not to chase your dreams—

NADIA: I gave up dreamin',
So I could have you come home to me…
Gave up being a teacher, so I could be a wife to you.
Got people around here, so scare of you, they scared of
me.
Ain't nobody going to hire me to teach their children…
Look, I'm not trying to argue with you.
Things just don't seem right to me when you bring his
name into matters.

CHRISTOPHER: Just wait and see…
I'm going to be a fine businessman just like Mr Berry…
Wear a velvet waistcoat, like him too.
Have people see me different for a change.

NADIA: I don't want to be married to a businessman…
I want to be married to you,
That's enough for me—

CHRISTOPHER: Not for me, baby…
I worked layin' bricks for seven years.
I'm more than that. We're more than that.
Think about it, that hotel could set us for life.
Come here… Give me your hands?
(*He takes* NADIA's *hands.*)
(*He kisses each one of her fingers.*)
Baby, aren't you tired of scrubbing floors,
Aren't you tired of caring all day for old, crusty,
wrinkled white women that don't know your name,
hardly remember their own?

NADIA: I've been cleanin' up for others all my life.

CHRISTOPHER: If I can get everything to come together, baby, believe me.
You'll never have to worry about something like that ever again...
Just a few months at Widow Luckey's and I'll be able to afford to go into business with Edwin.
Finally find a way to fit in to this world, for once.
Finally be able to put meat on this table instead of beans and rice.
Maybe if I do this right, I can buy you a proper ring.

(NADIA *sighs, picks up her basket and prepares to leave.*)

NADIA: Christopher C Davis, why can't you see?
I don't need those things. Ain't never needed those things.
I got to get going now, Miss Carol gonna be expectin' me...
I got to get ready for work.

CHRISTOPHER: Alright, then let me help you.

(CHRISTOPHER *and* NADIA *kiss.*)

(WARD *appears.*)

WARD: I'm trying to help you—

CHRISTOPHER: Nadia—

NADIA: Yeah?

CHRISTOPHER: I love you more than life itself.

NADIA: I know.

CHRISTOPHER: I'd die if I ever hurt you.

(*Jail cell.* CHRISTOPHER *sits...*)

WARD: I can't help you if you don't tell me what I need to know.

CHRISTOPHER: What makes you think you can help me?

You planning on holding off a mob?

WARD: I can help you if you let me help you.
I can hide you…I can protect you—

CHRISTOPHER: Protect me? You want to protect me?
How you going to do that?
I got a proposal, how about this?

WARD: I'm listening.

CHRISTOPHER: I'm not going to get justice here,
We both know it…
How about you let me go…
Close your eyes,
Be blind for an hour,
Let me slide out the back way towards freedom.

WARD: I can't do that, and you know it.

CHRISTOPHER: Truth is you don't got no intentions of
lettin' me outta here.

WARD: Damn right.

CHRISTOPHER: Then we have nothing to talk about.

WARD: I just want you to confess boy.

CHRISTOPHER: And I want you to see me.

WARD: See you?

(EDWIN enters.)

EDWIN: Yes, sir, I can see it now—

CHRISTOPHER: See me as a man. Just as a man—

EDWIN: Will you just take a look that boy.

CHRISTOPHER: Nothing else matters other than that.

EDWIN: One gotta love this country and what it willing
to give us,

CHRISTOPHER: Living, dying…loving…

EDWIN: When we're willing to sacrifice.

CHRISTOPHER: All that don't mean nothing if I can't ever be seen,
As a man… Cause that's all I'll ever be.
Just like you.
A man with wants and needs…Desires.
I want you to see that.

WARD: It's your life on the line, so talk.

CHRISTOPHER: You see it was all Edwin Berry's idea… that I start working for Widow Luckey.
He probably don't realize how much,
He got me tangled in things like they are now… or did he see it all along?

(EDWIN *and* CHRISTOPHER *stand looking upward at a vacant building.*)

CHRISTOPHER: The future site of Hotel Berry…

EDWIN: Yes sir, I can see it all clear as day.
Amazing building isn't it?
You know…I was thinking about you the other day.
I wouldn't be at this point if it wasn't for you.
Probably still be laying bricks and washing dishes.
If it wasn't for you… Well…
You may have thought I'd forgotten.
But I remember it clearly.
I remember that day you was working construction with me,
It was your first day there.
You were nothing but a boy,
Tall, knobby-kneed and big eyed, big headed teenager and I saw you.
Standing there with a one brick in your hand
Anyone could tell it was your first day on the job.
I approached you to help you out and you looked at me.

Looked at me with those eyes,
You placed that brick in my hand and you said to me.
You will build greatness one brick at a time.
I went home that day and gave it some thinking over.
That brick you handed me sat there by my bed that
night.
Tossed and turned… Sweated the night away…
I woke up the next day and I decided…
I decided I wasn't going to build no longer for
somebody else…but for me. I thank you for that…I
thank you for your friendship.

(Silence)

CHRISTOPHER: No.

EDWIN: You ain't even heard what I had to say—

CHRISTOPHER: You aren't foolin' nobody.
You want something, just come out and say it.

EDWIN: Look at me again like you did that day.

CHRISTOPHER: No…I told you before, it don't work that
way.
You want your fate read, go to a fortune teller.

EDWIN: I just need to know if my dream of this hotel
will be realized.

CHRISTOPHER: I don't need to look into you to see it.
Edwin.

EDWIN: Yeah boy.

CHRISTOPHER: Something just don't seems right, about
how we're going about this.

EDWIN: What are you talking about?
There's no such thing as right and wrong…
There's simply just is…

CHRISTOPHER: Edwin, I'm just—

EDWIN: Look towards the bigger picture, boy.
Picture it, boy, picture it. See what I see.
Twenty two room.
For now, but then it'll be fifty rooms.
And fifty rooms will turn to ninety
It'll be exquisite.
Electric call bells, electric lighting,
A hot water heating system and…
A bible in every room.
It'll be the beacon of sophistication, for this city.
It will be the finest hotel in all of Ohio.
Owned by a colored gent named, Mr Edwin C Berry…
With you by my side of course.
All I need is a loan from the bank and everything is
everything.
Can you see it?
(Silence)
What the hell's wrong with you, boy?

CHRISTOPHER: Nothing. I've just been thinking.

(Pause)

EDWIN: About?

CHRISTOPHER: Maybe there's another way to get that
loan other than through that woman.

(Silence)

EDWIN: I don't even know what to say to that.

CHRISTOPHER: Something just don't feel right about
using Widow Luckey.

EDWIN: Okay, now you've caught my full attention.
Let me tell you something, boy.
You have visions and so do I.
The only difference is that mine is a eighteen hundred
dollar vision…

So unless I magically stumble upon a signature on that loan, Or you get threee hundred dollars to pay a portion on the cost for this vision, You stay the damn course.

CHRISTOPHER: Edwin.

EDWIN: Don't Edwin me.
Use your head, boy.
Don't you want a better life for yourself? For Nadia?

CHRISTOPHER: Yes but not this way.

EDWIN: What other way is there...and why do you care? She's nothing.

CHRISTOPHER: She got troubles in her heart.

EDWIN: Who?

CHRISTOPHER: Widow Luckey.

EDWIN: Now I know you have lost your damn mind.

CHRISTOPHER: I'm just sayin'...I can see her pain.

EDWIN: You're causing me pain.

CHRISTOPHER: That woman has troubles.

EDWIN: I hear exactly what you're saying, but...
Don't be a damn fool, boy.
What does it matter to you whether she got troubles?
Troubles... What troubles?
She's white...
What she know about troubles?
She don't know nothing about having troubles...
I got troubles...you got troubles...
Look, boy, I know you have a good heart...
But... This is a small town.
A fragile town...
You can do that "let me look you in the eyes" stuff
with our people... but boy—

CHRISTOPHER: Edwin—

EDWIN: Don't matter to those people what your intentions are Stranger,
Your desire to help people will get you killed.
I don't want to see that, my friend—

CHRISTOPHER: I hear you… but—

EDWIN: But nothing.
Think about Nadia.
She gave up a lot for you boy.
How many educated colored women you see in this town married to a damn field hand?
Think about what kind of life you could provide her.
How the world sees you defines you.
Think about how the world would look at you two once you're able to parade around here and say you own something.
Once you have in your hands the keys to something.
Can you see that?
(Pause)
And guess what? It's simple to obtain.
All you got to do is keep your eyes down.
Smile and nod and do the job that is required of you and that's all.
That task is simple enough.
Can you do that?

CHRISTOPHER: Yeah

EDWIN: What?

CHRISTOPHER: Yeah.

EDWIN: I'm getting old, hearing not quite like it use to be.
So I'm going to ask you again.
Can you do that?
(Pause)

CHRISTOPHER: Yeah. I can do that.

EDWIN: Good. Just remember what you're doing this job for.

(LUCINDA *enters, she carries several packages.*)

(LUCINDA's *home. It's afternoon.*)

(CHRISTOPHER *is hard at work, he sings to himself a slow mournful song, when* LUCINDA *enters…*)

CHRISTOPHER: (*Singing*)
Somewhere in the garden of Eden…
A tree stands twisted…
Somewhere in the garden of Eden…
A tree stands twisted… A tree stands twisted…

LUCINDA: Stranger…Stranger, where are you?

CHRISTOPHER: Afternoon, looks like you got your hands tied—

LUCINDA: Didn't you hear me callin' you?

CHRISTOPHER: Sorry ma'am…

LUCINDA: And what did I tell you about callin' me, ma'am…
Give me a hand here.

CHRISTOPHER: What you got there?
You planning a trip, Mrs Luckey?

LUCINDA: No, why do you ask?

(CHRISTOPHER *pulls out a magazine from her package.*)

CHRISTOPHER: *Journal to the Greater World.*

LUCINDA: Oh, that…
That's my business, I'd thank you to keep out of it.

(*Pause*)

CHRISTOPHER: I figured it's lonely around here,
Not havin' anyone to talk to but if you don't want to talk…

Then I guess you don't have to talk.

(Silence)

LUCINDA: It's nothing…
Silly dreams that's all…
Just like to imagine the world outside of the Valley
Seems so grand the world beyond this place.

CHRISTOPHER: Life in this Valley is the only thing I've ever known.

LUCINDA: This place strangles you cause there is nothing here.
The world is out there…
Even what might seem like the small things are so grand,
Outside of this place.
Why in this magazine, they say that there is this amusement park attraction in old Parie, France…
That's French for Paris, France,
That's in Europe.

CHRISTOPHER: I'm aware of where France is, Mrs. Luckey.

LUCINDA: Anyhow this magazine has a way of making everything seem so heavenly.
Says when you first experience the attraction,
You feel a state of bliss,
That the ride will cause your heart to beat faster,
And your breathing gets faster from all the excitement and you feel this amazing rush all over.
Exciting the way they describe the ride.
Don't you think?

(CHRISTOPHER looks at LUCINDA. She looks at him.)

(Silence)

LUCINDA:I swear, the way you look at me.

(She places the magazine back into her bags.)

CHRISTOPHER: Sorry, Mrs Luckey.

LUCINDA: Is my hair misplaced?
I forget how much a walk it is from town.

CHRISTOPHER: No, you look beautiful, Mrs Luckey.

LUCINDA: That's good to hear, helps me forget I'm getting old.

CHRISTOPHER: You're not old in my eyes though.
Not how I see you.

LUCINDA: What exactly are you seeing?

CHRISTOPHER: Nothing, I apologize.

LUCINDA: Is it true you can see into people's souls?

*(*CHRISTOPHER *looks at* LUCINDA. *She looks at him.)*

LUCINDA: What do you see when you look at me?

(Pause)

CHRISTOPHER: That you're missing something in your life.

LUCINDA: What else?

CHRISTOPHER: Nothing…
I appreciate you hiring me.

LUCINDA: Well, I appreciate you, too.
Beautiful day isn't it.

CHRISTOPHER: It is… Storms approaching soon though.
I can sense it.

LUCINDA: Curious, what's it like when you have those…
Those visions of yours?

CHRISTOPHER: I should be getting back to work—

LUCINDA: Stranger, wait please.

CHRISTOPHER: I don't rightly know how to explain it
really.

LUCINDA: Try? Please.

(*Silence*)

CHRISTOPHER: I don't know when it'll come over me,
A fire starts over me…and it grows quiet at first,
My heart pounding hard the only thing I can hear.
And then that's when it begins.

LUCINDA: What begins?

CHRISTOPHER: The music…
I hear the music start to play.
It's filled with this kind of sorrow and pain that's
calling out to me.
Then flashes of images cut into me deep, twist around
me, and through me.
Each one worse than the next and as fast as that vision
arrives…
It's gone again and I find myself feeling at peace…
At peace in the quiet.
That quiet, I…I live for that moment.

LUCINDA: I see.

(*Silence*)

CHRISTOPHER: I really should be getting back to work,
Mrs Luckey.

LUCINDA: Must you go?
Stay awhile. I don't get much company nowadays.
Talk with me.
Stranger?

CHRISTOPHER: Yes, Mrs Luckey?

LUCINDA: I'm curious, everybody in town knows you
as Stranger, why is that?

CHRISTOPHER: What makes you ask that?

LUCINDA: Curiosity…
Loneliness…
Those two combined will get anybody into trouble.

CHRISTOPHER: My mother, gave it to me—

LUCINDA: You're mother named you, Stranger?

CHRISTOPHER: Honest—

LUCINDA: If you don't want to tell me you can just
simply say so.

CHRISTOPHER: We lived in a small little cottage…
Small, weather beaten, dust floor cottage.
I'd be readin' my lessons for the day,
Didn't get proper schoolin' like the others around here,
My mother taught herself how to read.
Had me learn for myself, day after day,
The Bible, Shakespeare
There I would be sittin' on the kitchen floor,
Waitin' for her to come back from work and her daily
errands.
I'd see her trudging on down the road.
Weary, tired from long hours of hard labor.
And I'd rise to my feet,
Standin' behind the screen door,
Watchin'…
Just watchin' her slowly make her way toward home.
That weariness, that sadness on the face of your
mother,
That's something a man will never forget.
And when I'd run out that door, to go to her.
Arms outstretched wide.
I'd see that a change would come…
A change would come over her.
She'd change in that moment.
From tired worker woman to a queen, just like that.

Same worn sweat drenched clothes,
Same salt and peppered hair, same faced kissed by the
sun
a thousand time too many to count.
But there was something…
Something would always change in her.
Something beautiful.
Every time she'd see me… something in her eyes.
Something in the way… in the way she'd look at me.
And she'd smile when I embraced her,
Clutched tightly to her.
And she would say to me,
Hey there Stranger!
Hey there you beautiful boy, you beautiful man,
you beautiful stranger.
I see you.
Stuck with me ever since.
Funny though of all the people to call me Stranger,
Nobody could ever see me like she did.
I never told nobody that before.

LUCINDA: She sounds like a wonderful woman.

CHRISTOPHER: She was…
I've been lookin' all my life, for a woman just like her.

LUCINDA: Have you found one?

CHRISTOPHER: Yes, Mrs Luckey, I believe I have…

LUCINDA: How does she make you feel?

CHRISTOPHER: She's my peace…

LUCINDA: I hope you let her know that.
I envy that feeling.

CHRISTOPHER: Love her more than life itself.
Sometimes I regret she loves me…
She threw away her dreams in place of mine.

Dreams shouldn't be sacrificed for love.

LUCINDA: There's no sacrifice greater in my opinion...
(Pause)
Have you heard Edwin is trying to build a hotel here?

CHRISTOPHER: Oh yes, Mr Berry is building the finest
hotel in not just this town but all of Ohio. And I'm
going to his partner for that.

LUCINDA: I thought that was just another one of
Edwin's crazy schemes.

CHRISTOPHER: Oh it's not crazy at all.
It's going to be what this town needs.
Electric call bells, electric lighting, arches and more.

LUCINDA: That sounds unimaginable.
(She laughs.)

CHRISTOPHER: Oh, you just got to open your eyes to the
possibilities, That's all you got to do. See what others
can't see—

(WARD enters at the door, white petal flowers in his hand.)

WARD: Good afternoon, Mr. Luckey.
Stranger, it's a surprise to see you here.
I didn't know—

LUCINDA: Yes, I recently hired him.

WARD: Did you now?

CHRISTOPHER: I should get back to work.
(He turns to exit.)

LUCINDA: Stranger, wait...

CHRISTOPHER: Yes, Mrs Luckey?

(LUCINDA hands CHRISTOPHER the magazine.)

LUCINDA: Hold on to it, give it a look.
Maybe it'll help open your eyes.
Let me know what you think.

CHRISTOPHER: I'll do that... Thank you.

WARD: Me and you need to have a little talk later, Stranger.

(CHRISTOPHER *exits*.)

LUCINDA: Sheriff Ward—

WARD: Please call me, Timothy...

LUCINDA: What a surprise.

WARD: These are for you.

LUCINDA: Flowers...

WARD: I thought you might like them.
Stranger, really?

LUCINDA: Yes, he is a tremendous help around here.

WARD: Was I interrupting anything?

LUCINDA: No... Oh mercy, no...

(Pause)

WARD: I meant nothing by it... My apologies.

LUCINDA: I'm going to pretend that you didn't enter my house and insult my virtue.

(WARD *takes a breath*.)

WARD: Did I mention that I brought you flower?

(Silence)

LUCINDA: It's been a while since I had flowers.

WARD: I used to bring you flowers.

LUCINDA: I don't remember.

WARD: Ah, you remember.
I was but a boy, I had brought you flowers, white ones like these.
Hand picked...
I found you afterschool one day

I was about ten years old…
I had every intention to have you, as Mrs. Ward.
I approached you dressed in my Sunday's best.

LUCINDA: Seems like another life, then
Lord, knows I was such a cruel child.
When you presented me the flowers, I do recall…
Correct me if I'm wrong.
But, I pushed you into the mud at school, and chased
you home throwing rocks at you all the way.
I am terribly sorry…
I was just a school girl with a silly infatuation,
And that was my way of showing it.

WARD: That was then.

LUCINDA: And this is now.
Lord, knows time was simpler then.
Children don't know anything about love,
Or hate,
Or jealousy…
About being alone…They just are…

WARD: It's a beautiful day isn't it?
There is just something about this season.

LUCINDA: There certainly is—

WARD: I got a while before I have to make my rounds.
I'd like your company.
Would you sit with me?

LUCINDA: This is a rather unexpected surprise but I'd
be honored.
If I'd known you were coming by, I would've boil us
some tea.

WARD: Oh, think nothing of it.
I was just riding along the river and saw these flowers
Said to myself, I ought to pick me a few,

Bring'em your way.

LUCINDA: I'm blushing…thank you.

(WARD *whistles*.)

WARD: My word… My word…my word…
What a great view of the South Bridge you have from here.
You remember how we once looked out towards this bridge together.

LUCINDA: Timothy, don't.

WARD: Sorry…Lucinda?

LUCINDA: Yes.

WARD: If I might be so bold,
Now that there is no puddles of mud around,
No rocks to hurl at me…
Lucinda, I'd like to…
I liked to come by every now and then…and check on you.

LUCINDA: You'd like to what?
I don't know,
Sheriff, my loving husband has been in the ground,
No longer than a few months time,
and I find your attempts to court me—

WARD: Purely want to make sure you're doing alright.

LUCINDA: I see, why the sudden interest in my well-being?

WARD: Always been interested… You know that just as well as I do.
With your husband's death and all.
And you are living in this house by yourself.
You shouldn't be living like this…Alone.
Woman needs man.
Man needs woman.

And I...
I just want to make sure you're well taken care of.
It's the least I could do—

LUCINDA: Well I'll have you know, Sheriff, I'm far from alone.

WARD: You're not alone?

LUCINDA: Not alone in the least bit.
I have company, lots of company.
Just yesterday the women of the church came by for tea.

WARD: Really?

LUCINDA: And Stranger been coming by everyday to do work.
So you see I'm not alone...not alone at all.

WARD: Well...I see... You don't need that boy around, there's a man here now.
I can come by help around your house for you.
When you need me...of course.
Save you the hassle of having to pay him all the time.

LUCINDA: That's quite nice of you...
But Stranger, manages well enough for me.

WARD: Still I'm...I'm more than available to—

LUCINDA: To what?

WARD: To keep you company if you'd like.

LUCINDA: I'll keep that in mind.

WARD: This is a small town, Lucinda—

LUCINDA: Timothy, I'm going to pretend my ignorance and ask,
What does that mean?

WARD: Well... As I said this is a small town.
And small towns like to talk.

For instance, I know the dignified ladies of the church,
Haven't come by since your husband passed…
God rest his soul.
And I've known for awhile now through town
gossip…
That you've ain't had company in quite awhile…
Far as anybody knows nobody has come by to you pay
a visit.

LUCINDA: Well…I…I prefer my own company.

WARD: Lucinda—

LUCINDA: Timothy—

WARD: Just say you'll consider it.
Consider my company.
You know me…Know me better than most.
I'm sure if you just look into my soul,
You'd see that I'm a good man, and an ambitious man.
One of these days I'm going to be mayor of this town.
I just want to come by and see you every now and
then…

LUCINDA: See me…

WARD: As I said before strickly, for your well being of
course.

LUCINDA: I should be going in now,
I have some pressing matters to attend to,
I hope you understand.

WARD: Of course, have yourself a pleasant evening,
flower.

(LUCINDA *exits.*)

(CHRISTOPHER *enters.*)

WARD: Stranger…
You stop and look at me when I'm talking to you.

(CHRISTOPHER *stops, turns.*)

CHRISTOPHER: Yes, sir?

WARD: I'm keeping a close eye on you. A very close eye on you.

(He panics and flees.)

(As the vision intensifies music plays and CHRISTOPHER *is bathed in bright lights, it's blinding.)*

(Night… Home. CHRISTOPHER *finds himself standing outside, he hums to himself.)*

*(*NADIA *stands watching him.)*

NADIA: What you doing out here?

CHRISTOPHER: Watching the sky… Seems like a dark storm is brewing.

NADIA: Well it's a long way from here if it is.

CHRISTOPHER: I'm sorry I didn't wake you did I?

NADIA: You plan on sleepin' anytime soon?

CHRISTOPHER: Just doing some thinkin', I'll be in soon.

NADIA: What's wrong?

CHRISTOPHER: Why something always got to be wrong?

NADIA: Well?

CHRISTOPHER: Well what?

NADIA: Well what's wrong?

CHRISTOPHER: Nothin' wrong.

NADIA: You sure?

CHRISTOPHER: Yes

NADIA: Is there anything I can do?

CHRISTOPHER: No—

NADIA: Nothing's bothering you?

CHRISTOPHER: Besides you—

(NADIA *smacks* CHRISTOPHER *on the back of the head.*)

CHRISTOPHER: Woman, will you stop that—

NADIA: Don't make me beat you, Christopher C
Davis…
I'm tryin' to help you.
You're pacing…you only pace when something is
wrong.

CHRISTOPHER: I'm fine, Nadia.

NADIA: Then why aren't you asleep?

CHRISTOPHER: Cause I can't sleep.

NADIA: I'm your wife…
Tell me.

CHRISTOPHER: There's no point frettin' over it—

NADIA: It's that nightmare about the old woman again?

CHRISTOPHER: No, this dream was different this time…
Started off with me in the home of the Jenkin's family.
Lookin' at that baby entangled in his crib, stranglin'.
I move to help the baby…
Next thing I know I find that I'm standing under a
twisted tree, tangled in weeds…Strangling me.
And in the darkness I see eyes staring back at me…
and I can't see into them.

NADIA: It was just a dream.

CHRISTOPHER: You don't understand, love…
It felt…it seemed real…
Those eyes just looking at me…
Every night that dream gets more and more real to me.
Wake up barely able to breathe…
Tonight, I even thought I saw the old woman,
over by the clearing watching me.
She's coming for me…
I can feel her coming…

NADIA: Come here…

CHRISTOPHER: What?

NADIA: Don't "what?" me…
Give me your hands—
(She takes his hands.)
You're hands are trembling…

CHRISTOPHER: They're getting worse, Nadia—

(NADIA kisses each one of CHRISTOPHER's fingers.)

NADIA: Come to bed, before you catch your death out here.
Come on. Come to bed.
I'm here for you, Stranger…

(NADIA cradles CHRISTOPHER.)

CHRISTOPHER: I'm scared, baby.

NADIA: I know. I know.
(Singing)
There will be peace in the valley for me, some day
There will be peace in the valley for me, oh Lord I pray
There'll be no sadness, no sorrow
No trouble, trouble I see
There will be peace in the valley for me, for me

(Lights fade, come up on LUCINDA's home. Noon)

(CHRISTOPHER with hatchet in hand down center)

(He's been hard at work shirtless. He wipes his brow.)

LUCINDA: Stranger?

CHRISTOPHER: You alright, ma'am?

LUCINDA: I'm…I'm fine…
Could you perhaps put on a shirt…for just a moment?
What are you doing it's November?

CHRISTOPHER: So hot out here when your working…

(CHRISTOPHER *turns and* LUCINDA *notices the scars upon his back.*)

LUCINDA: Oh, dear God…
How'd you get those scars on your back?

(*Silence*)

CHRISTOPHER: Your right, I should put my shirt on.

LUCINDA: Honestly, Stranger, what happened to your back?

CHRISTOPHER: Sorry, Miss Luckey.
I won't have my shirt off again…
If you got the time,
I want to talk to you about an opportunity you might take an interest in… About the hotel.

LUCINDA: Maybe later alright.
Stranger, before I forget…
Thank you for fixin' that roof up there…
You did a nice job with that.

CHRISTOPHER: Thank you, ma'am…

LUCINDA: Before you finish up today that tree out there needs to be cut down.
I need some more firewood, before the winter comes our way.
It's supposed to be a long one, I've been told.

CHRISTOPHER: I'll get on it, right away Mrs Luckey.

LUCINDA: Stranger?

(CHRISTOPHER *looks at* LUCINDA. *She looks at him.*)

(*Silence…*)

LUCINDA: There's one more thing, I want from you…

CHRISTOPHER: Yes, Mrs Luckey.

(*Silence*)

LUCINDA: I don't know how to ask this but…

I need you to see inside of my soul.

(Silence)

CHRISTOPHER: No, Mrs Luckey.

LUCINDA: No?

CHRISTOPHER: No.
(Pause)
It doesn't work that way.

(Silence)

LUCINDA: If you look at me.
If you take a look into my eyes then…
I'll listen to your proposal about the hotel.

CHRISTOPHER: You'll let me talk to you about the hotel?

LUCINDA: I will.

(Silence)

CHRISTOPHER: It just comes. I don't know when it happens it just—

LUCINDA: Try please.
That's all I'm asking. Just try. Just try for me.
(Pause)
Cause I'm empty inside and maybe…
I don't know.
Can you just try for me, please?

(Silence…)

(CHRISTOPHER begins to speak. His words flow from him in a fevered state. His entire essence seems as if he's been set afire.)

CHRISTOPHER: I see you, Lucinda Luckey…
I see your pain…
I see your loneliness—
It's all twisted up, entangled around your soul.

I see your loneliness wrapping around your heart, and
spread through your veins chokin' you.
I see you, sitting in your rocking chair by the fireplace,
Gazing out towards the Southbridge on cold nights.
I see your tears staining your dress.
You miss the sound of your children's laughter in your
house.
Your wedding night you ran away from your husband.
Made it as far as the Southbridge before
He found you hiding under the branches of an old tree.
Kickin' and screamin', He carried you back to your
wedding bed.

LUCINDA: How could you know that?—

CHRISTOPHER: I see you Lucinda…
I see your pain…
I see your anguish…
I see you crying your eyes out,
Arms outstretched wide to God.
I can you see your children… I see you.
I see a lover's scorned, a child born, a bride's lie…
I see your children
I see their graves—

LUCINDA: Please stop you're scaring me—

CHRISTOPHER: I see you…I see your loneliness…
I see this house,
I see a shadow over the valley starting to form,
Like a storm is approaching.
A storm that will take a long time before it ever finds a
calms—

LUCINDA: Stop it please—

CHRISTOPHER: I see you…I see you…I see you!!!

LUCINDA: STOP IT PLEASE!!!

(CHRISTOPHER *and* LUCINDA *look at each other, really looking at each other.)*

CHRISTOPHER: *(Shocked)* It's never happened like that before…
It's never happened like that before.
(To LUCINDA*)*
I…I'm sorryI didn't mean to hurt you,
That wasn't my intention at all.
(He moves towards her.)

LUCINDA: Don't touch me… don't touch me.
How could you see all of that?
I don't understand.

CHRISTOPHER: Lucinda don't cry
You don't have to cry anymore, that's what I'm saying—

LUCINDA: You saw all that?

CHRISTOPHER: Stop cryin', alright…please…
Can you do that for me?
Can you—

(CHRISTOPHER *and* LUCINDA *look at each other.)*

(They kiss…)

CHRISTOPHER: We shouldn't.

(CHRISTOPHER *and* LUCINDA *kiss…)*

LUCINDA: It's not proper…
It's not right…
It could find us the kind of trouble,
Neither of us needs in our lives.

(Silence. CHRISTOPHER *and* LUCINDA *want to pull away but can't.)*

LUCINDA: I'm a widow… Men don't look at me in that way.

(Silence)

CHRISTOPHER: Maybe they should?

LUCINDA: You can't… We can't…People will talk.

(EDWIN enters unseen to CHRISTOPHER and LUCINDA. He watches for moment before he turns and leaves.)

CHRISTOPHER: No one will know—

LUCINDA: You don't know what you're saying,
This is something we can't get tangled up into…

(CHRISTOPHER and LUCINDA kiss…)

(He stops and pulls away.)

CHRISTOPHER: We can't.
I should go.

(CHRISTOPHER turns to leave and LUCINDA pulls him close to her.)

LUCINDA: Shhh…I just need you to see me…

(CHRISTOPHER pulls LUCINDA into him, wrapping her arms around his neck, entangling her with him. She tightens her grip around him. They kiss.   )

END OF ACT ONE

Interlude

*(A singular red light pierces through the darkness of the
stage revealing* CHRISTOPHER *standing atop a tree stump.
Indistinct whispers. He stands half naked arms outstretched.
He hums a mournful pain filled song softly to himself, as if
in heartbroken mourning.)*

CHRISTOPHER: Can you see me?

*(*CHRISTOPHER *begins humming the same haunting tune
again as the lights dim swallowing him into the darkness.)*

(Black out)

ACT TWO:
Book of Memories Torn

(LUCINDA's *house. Same day, evening.* CHRISTOPHER *and* LUCINDA.)

(*They dress…*)

(LUCINDA *touches his back tracing the length of his scars.*)

LUCINDA: (*Sings*)
Somewhere in the garden of Eden…
A tree stands twisted…
Somewhere in the garden of Eden…
A tree stands twisted.
I've never heard that song before,
It's haunting.
Where'd you learn it?

CHRISTOPHER: An old woman sung it to me once.

LUCINDA: Those scars on your back,
Look almost like that tree over by the Southbridge,
The way the scars move up your spine, and branch out,
All twisted like.

CHRISTOPHER: It's ugly.

(CHRISTOPHER *attempts to cover the scars with his shirt and* LUCINDA *stops him. She kisses the length of his scars.*)

LUCINDA: I think they're beautiful, it's our scars that define us.

CHRISTOPHER: I should get going, Lucinda—

LUCINDA: Please, Christopher, wait—

CHRISTOPHER: I don't do this—

LUCINDA: Stay just a while longer,
Would you like some tea or coffee perhaps.
I have some of my husband's whiskey if you like.

CHRISTOPHER: I'm fine. Thank you—

LUCINDA: Why are you pacing about like that?

CHRISTOPHER: It's nothing.

LUCINDA: Sit, please…

(CHRISTOPHER *sits down.*)

CHRISTOPHER: I should be getting on my way.

LUCINDA: I want to understand.
These visions…
How can you see the way you do?

(Silence)

CHRISTOPHER: It was the old woman.

LUCINDA: The Old Woman?

CHRISTOPHER: I was in the farm house stable working
as a child,
When an old woman came in hummin'…looked at me.
Waved me on over to follow her.
And I did, don't know why, just did.
I still remember that old woman, see her in my dreams.
She had a look on her face.
Her eyes, I ain't ever seen eyes like that.
Seemed like every drop of tears in that old woman's
body had been wept outta her.
She took my little hand and guided me on down to this
clearing at the end of the property to an old ash tree.

Old and twisted from time and there I saw a man legs just danglin'.

His hands tied behind his back.

And flies fat from feedin' off his misery circled him.

I looked up into his vacant eyes and they looked back at me.

Accusing me.

I wanted to run, wanted to leave that place and not look back but I couldn't…

My feet was rooted to the earth…

After a moment I found that the man swinging by the neck…

Had disappeared.

Faded away into the afternoon sun.

When I looked around saw the same with the old woman too.

Gone…

I found myself standing there still in that stable.

I had never left, but something was different about me.

Had these scar upon my back, marking me for life.

Every morning I wake up to find a new scar upon me.

But I could feel something else as well…

This pressure as if a rope was tightening around my neck.

And I was struggling to breathe.

Feel it everyday I wake up.

Feel it every time I walk down these streets.

Feel it every time I look into someone's eyes.

Like I was being strangled by something I can't see.

Something I can never cut loose.

LUCINDA: To think you were just a child when that happened.

To be given that kind of weight upon your shoulders.

CHRISTOPHER: Wish everyday of my life, I never took that woman's hand…
That's a memory I wish I never had.

LUCINDA: Memories and history are supposed to be brought back up,
It's how we keep from forgetting.
Who am I to throw away the bad memories and keep only the good?
We need both to heal our scars.

CHRISTOPHER: Some scars I don't think ever heal.

LUCINDA: True.
Old Man Luckey.
Always smiling and laughing,
Laughing and smiling,
I learned to hate that laugh and his smile…

CHRISTOPHER: Again, I'm sorry if I brought up painful memories.

LUCINDA: It's those memories that define us.

CHRISTOPHER: I should be gettin' going—

LUCINDA: May I ask you something else?

CHRISTOPHER: My wife…
She'll be worried sick, wonderin' where I am.

LUCINDA: I'm makin' dinner, if you're interested…

CHRISTOPHER: It's getting' kinda late.

LUCINDA: It'll be done in just a few… Some candied yams—
And a side of some bread and butter pudding.

CHRISTOPHER: I'd like to take you up on that.

LUCINDA: I'm roastin' a skewer of hen stuffed with sausage—

CHRISTOPHER: Look, honestly, I wish I could stay—

LUCINDA: Then you should… Have supper with me,
Christopher,
That's all I'm askin'…
And go on back home to that young gal, waitin' for
you.
She'll understand.
All that food is just going to go to waste otherwise.
I've gotten so use to cookin' for two.
I don't…the house… It gets…
I'd really appreciate your company.
Have someone to talk to.
You can tell me about this hotel you and Edwin Berry
are dreaming up.
I just don't want to be alone in silence,
Just for awhile.
I'd like that.
I'd like for someone to see me for once.

(*Lights up on* CHRISTOPHER *and* WARD, *stage left in jail.*)

WARD: Lies!!! Lies!!! Lies!!!
I see right through you.
You don't think I can't see you lying to me?

CHRISTOPHER: Why would I lie?

(*The sound of the mob growing closer.*)

WARD: You just don't get this do you?
Hear those voices gathering outside, huh?
Do you know what that's the sound of?
That my friend…
That is the sound of civic minded men that have had
enough.
That is the sound of men, who go to work every day,
To put food on their children's plate…
Good Christian men… And they're thirsty…
Parched more like it…at my door right now…

Demandin' themselves justice—

CHRISTOPHER: Justice or nigra blood?

WARD: It's pretty much the same thing in they book…
To them one taste just a little sweeter than the other—

CHRISTOPHER: You don't believe me.

WARD: No I don't damnit.

CHRISTOPHER: You don't like the truth.
Most people don't…
They'd rather wrap up the truth with lies.

(WARD *takes a drink from his flask.*)

WARD: I'm trying to help you…
Where's your conscience.

CHRISTOPHER: That word conscience, it makes me wonder.
Why you want to help me so bad?
What's the truth behind that, huh?

WARD: I know what you're doing—

CHRISTOPHER: Do you?

WARD: Yeah, you're a smart one.
You know a lesser man could let that mob hang you after you told that lie;
From my understanding there's thirty-forty guns out there.
Some came from as far away as Albany.
But I want a jury to find you guilty.
I want to have that pleasure to carry with me.

CHRISTOPHER: What else you carrying with you…
Mind tellin' me that sheriff?

WARD: You might have the town believing you got some kinda sight.
But you don't got me fooled?

CHRISTOPHER: I see you Sheriff Ward…
I see your guilt.
I see your sin… See it when I look in your eyes.
See your bare hands clenched tight
As you strike Lil' Sammy Boy…
Why'd you do it Sheriff?
Few drinks too many,
or did Lil' Sammy Boy just rub you wrong—

WARD: I don't know where you got your information.
But you're wrong about that—

CHRISTOPHER: I see your soul, Sheriff Ward—

WARD: Shut your mouth damnit.

CHRISTOPHER: You, Hess, and DeLoach had a good
time that night,
Celebrating you turning a year older,
I see you ambushing that boy in the darkness.

WARD: It didn't happen like that—

CHRISTOPHER: I see you…
I see the very crime that strangles your soul…
He planned to leave the valley.
Planned to oneday become an educated man at
Wilberforce
Why'd you do it sheriff? Tell me that?
Did you beat him because he was too bright…too
ambitious…
Or did you beat him just cause he was an Indian haired
black boy,
Who dreamed of leaving this valley—

WARD: I'm warning you—

CHRISTOPHER: I see you…
I see your rage…
He never saw it coming…

Never saw it coming as Hess knocked out his eye.
That's why you want to try to save me.
In hopes that you'll save your soul for a past sin,
By trying to save mine...
One life in exchange for another...I see you Sheriff.
For that one time
For that one eye
You let your moral compass point you wrong.
I see you and your guilt.
I see your guilt.
I see your guilt.

(WARD *grabs* CHRISTOPHER.)

(LUCINDA *appears.*)

WARD: My guilt... My guilt?!!
I'm not the one guilty of cheating on his wife, now am
I? —

LUCINDA: Wouldn't it be nice if we left this place—

WARD: You know you could make this easier?—

LUCINDA: We could go to Europe... See the greater
world—

WARD: Easier...on us both—

LUCINDA: Forget about investing in some silly hotel.

WARD: If you're not willin' to help yourself.

LUCINDA: A hotel here?

WARD: Maybe you'll be willin' to help—

LUCINDA: And you won't need to worry about Nadia—

WARD: I don't know...

LUCINDA: We could leave her some money,
Make sure she's well taken care of—

WARD: Maybe that beautiful bride of yours?

CHRISTOPHER: Leave her out of this.

WARD: Would you be willin' to help your wife by confessin'?
Think about it boy. Don't you get it?
I'm trying to save her the shame of seein' you swing from the neck?

LUCINDA: I'm simply saying she can't make you happy. Not like I can.

CHRISTOPHER: I said leave her out of this.

WARD: Well? I'd like to, Christopher…
But if you're not willin' to help yourself…
Well that leads me to wonder,
What are you willin' to sacrifice?

LUCINDA: I don't understand why you're acting like this.

WARD: Yes that's the question.

CHRISTOPHER: She's not involved in this.

WARD: I wonder if she ever looked you in the eyes…
Looked at you and saw what I see.

LUCINDA: Can't we just leave this place?

WARD: Think she ever looked at you with both eyes wide open?
And said to herself…
My God.
What is this standing next to me?

CHRISTOPHER: Stop.

WARD: Why?

LUCINDA: I upset you?

WARD: Bring her down over here, let her see you behind bars.

LUCINDA: Here you'll always be seen as less than you are.

WARD: Why should I not let her see you for who you are?

LUCINDA: A nothing…

WARD / LUCINDA: I'm giving you a chance,

LUCINDA: What can you possibly accomplish here, Christopher?

WARD / LUCINDA: Come on tell me that…

WARD: Tell me?

CHRISTOPHER: Go to hell.

WARD: Go to hell?
Those are bold words, boy.
They want to hang you,
And the only man standing between you and that angel called death is me, and you say go to hell?!!
That wife of yours—

LUCINDA: I need you Christopher…
It should be a clear choice…
Nadia can't offer you anything…
I can.

CHRISTOPHER: I said leave my wife's name out of this.
(*He rises to his feet.*)

WARD: Oh, that's the spirit…there you go…
You want to strike me, is that it?
Come on and strike me…
Hatchet's right there, go for it.
Attack me like you attacked Widow Luckey…
Bash my skull with that hatchet,
Like you did Lucinda Luckey, huh?
Oh if that pretty little wife of yours could see you now—

CHRISTOPHER: I'll kill you.

WARD: Lucinda Luckey get you mad too, is that what
happened?

(CHRISTOPHER *tries to charge for the hatchet.* WARD *does
the same.* CHRISTOPHER *wrestles the hatchet out of the
sheriff's grip and holds the hatchet to his throat.*)

CHRISTOPHER: Is this what you want to see, huh?
I could do it, you know that Sheriff?
Leave you here lying in your own damn blood,
as I sneak out the back way.
I could do it and not think twice about it.
But I ain't…
I'm man you hear me. A man.

(WARD, *after a struggle, wrestles* CHRISTOPHER *down. One
hand upon* CHRISTOPHER'*s throat,* WARD *raises the hatchet
high above his head and stops himself before he brings it
angrily down upon* CHRISTOPHER.)

(WARD *lets out a deep breath.*)

WARD: I'm not a perfect man, Stranger.
I got my sins that forever I'll be trying to amend.
Your wife…you know she's…I envy you for what you
got.

(NADIA *is by a window looking out, she's folding clothes,
and placing them into her basket.*)

NADIA: Do you know what time it is?

CHRISTOPHER: I know…I know…she's my blessing and
I don't deserve her.
Don't think I ever have really told her how much she
means to me…
(*He crosses right into the house.*)

NADIA: It's late—

CHRISTOPHER: I know…I'm sorry.
Want me to help you with the dishes, love?

NADIA: Where you been?

CHRISTOPHER: Workin' over at Lucinda's…
I mean Widow Luckey's place.

NADIA: Your food sittin' on the stove…it's cold.
I made rice and beans.

CHRISTOPHER: That's alright, Widow Luckey cooked.

NADIA: Oh, I see.

CHRISTOPHER: Any coffee in the pot?

NADIA: It's been getting cold.
That roof still needs mendin'…
Said a couple days ago, you was plannin' on mendin'
it.

CHRISTOPHER: I'll get on it.

NADIA: Widow Luckey, got to beg you to mend her
roof?

CHRISTOPHER: She payin' me, Nadia…she's payin' me.

NADIA: Well…I don't like her. I don't trust her—

CHRISTOPHER: She's good people—

NADIA: Jaysus said the same thing about the—

CHRISTOPHER: Jesus, love, not Jaysus.

NADIA: You say Jesus, I say Jaysus.

CHRISTOPHER: She's just a lonely woman—

NADIA: You find her attractive?—

CHRISTOPHER: She's all by herself up there—

NADIA: Do you find that woman you working for
attractive?

CHRISTOPHER: I love you, Nadia… Just let it be—

NADIA: It's a yes or no question…
So just answer it—

CHRISTOPHER: For a woman...
Her age.

NADIA: I knew it...I have it in my mind to just...
What else are you doing 'round her house?

CHRISTOPHER: Stop it—

NADIA: We need to talk—

CHRISTOPHER: Talkin' can wait, love, I'm tired, I'm
going to bed.

NADIA: Stranger?

CHRISTOPHER: You tell me what to do, cause I don't
know—

NADIA: It's just that I have a bad feeling, about all this.
And when I get these feeling,
I've learned over time to trust them.
Honestly, Christopher, I won't know what to do if—

CHRISTOPHER: I'm not going nowhere. I love you
alright...I love you, Nadia...
I don't know what I got to do to prove that.

NADIA: I love you, too Stranger, but-—

CHRISTOPHER: Nobody knows me like you do, love...

(CHRISTOPHER *and* NADIA *kiss.*)

NADIA: Then how come when I kiss you,
It don't feel like I'm kissing the man I fell in love with?
Can you tell me that?

(*Silence*)

(CHRISTOPHER *turns to leave.*)

NADIA: Where you going?

CHRISTOPHER: Out... If I see the man, you fell in love
with,
I'll tell him to come home.

NADIA: I need to talk to you, Christopher…
Christopher! Christopher!

*(Night…*CHRISTOPHER *moves towards the jail cell with* WARD.*)*

WARD: Have you heard a single thing I'm tellin' you?
Sign the confession, so I can appease this mob…

CHRISTOPHER: *(Reads)* I, Christopher C Davis, hereby
confess to committing the assault and performing
forced outrage upon the person of Lucinda Luckey.
I'm not signing this.
I'm innocent… Let me go.

WARD: I want to help you.

CHRISTOPHER: How confessin' guilt when I'm innocent
helpin'?—

WARD: Just sign the confession.
Let me show it to those men gathering outside.
Let me end this before it gets out of hand.

CHRISTOPHER: Either way I'm a dead man.

WARD: Have you ever witnessed a lynchin' before?—

*(*CHRISTOPHER *doesn't answer.)*

WARD: I seen one once.
They strung up five colored gents in front of the Posey
County Courthouse lawn in Indiana.
Tortured them slowly at first.
Men died screamin to God to save them…
Most inhuman thing I've ever seen in all my days.
See I'm just tryin' to spare you that kind of death.
Those men out there, are ready to kill you, boy…
They'll walk you four blocks down Court Street
And will hang you by the Southbridge…
Understand?

CHRISTOPHER: I can't sign that.

WARD: Sign it—

CHRISTOPHER: I can't.

WARD: Come on now—

CHRISTOPHER: I wouldn't harm a soul. I told you that—

WARD: Well we proved that otherwise earlier didn't we?

CHRISTOPHER: What about you?

(LUCINDA appears.)

LUCINDA: Hello sheriff…

WARD: What about me?

LUCINDA: I didn't expect you today.

CHRISTOPHER: My momma use to tell me if you've never considered murder,
Then you've never been in love.

(LUCINDA's… WARD approaches. CHRISTOPHER is working in the garden.)

WARD: You look beautiful today—

LUCINDA: Thank you.
Timothy have you been drinkin'?

WARD: I've had a nip here and there…Can I talk to you?

LUCINDA: I thought that's what we were doing?

(WARD moves towards LUCINDA.)

WARD: Take my hand.

(WARD offers his hand out to LUCINDA and she takes it.)

(He draws her close to him.)

WARD: Lucinda…Lucinda…Lucinda…
You are so beautiful.
A stunning piece of work, you know that.

In every way imaginable.
Everytime I see you
I just want to reach out and touch you.
You're so delicate…
So soft…
So pure…
(Pause)
Like a flower.
(He kisses her.)
I'm sorry I shouldn't have done that.

LUCINDA: Let go of me.

WARD: I'm sorry.

LUCINDA: I said, let go.

WARD: We could have a good life together now don't you think?

LUCINDA: Sheriff, I care for you…

WARD: And I for you.

LUCINDA: And I don't want to hurt you now…
You were a good man.

WARD: Were?

LUCINDA: You had a kindness you showed to everyone once.
A charm and wit about you.
But I don't see that man anymore.

WARD: I could be that man.

LUCINDA: You and I, we're not meant to be together.

WARD: I don't think you realize what you're saying.
I'm not one to turn away from.
I've held this love in my soul for you a long time…
Long time.

Don't you forget who you snuck off to love during our
youth.
Don't you forget who remained silent when the child
he could never claim died in the war…
I remained patient, and waited for that old fool to be
dead and buried in the ground.
Waited long, long time for you,
The love I've yearned for my entire life.
And now you deny me. You deny me.
Why? Tell me that—

LUCINDA: I'm sorry if I hurt you,
That's not my intentions,
I was a silly child then Timothy.
But not now…
The things that I held in my heart for you once…
The fire in my heart has died out for you.
It left my heart same day our…
(*Silence*)
I was wrong… We were wrong…
But you're a friend, a good friend.
And that's what I need right now nothing more.
I wish you could see that.

WARD: I wish you could see me as more…
When something happens and I pray nothing will…
You'll wish I was here for you.

LUCINDA: I need to go…

LUCINDA / WARD: I have/ pressing matters to attend
to…

WARD: Yes, I know…

LUCINDA: I'm sorry.

(WARD *notices* CHRISTOPHER.)

(*He reaches into his vest pocket pulls out an envelope.*)

WARD: You see this envelope?

CHRISTOPHER: I see it, sir. What do you want?

WARD: What do I want?
Not a matter of what I want…It's what you want…
You know what this is? This is three hundred dollars.
This is my campaign money for Mayor.
I want you to take this,
Take this and find a way out of Widow Luckey's
employment.

CHRISTOPHER: I don't think I want your money, sir.

WARD: I think you do…
You can do a lot with three hundred dollars.
That's freedom boy, right here in my hands…
Three hundred dollars can fulfill a lot of dreams.
Maybe invest in that hotel, Edwin been chattering on
about.
Maybe buy your wife something nice.
Get her a ring perhaps, give her a proper-like wedding.
(Silence)
Oh yes, boy, I know. Believe me I know.
What? You don't think my own flesh and blood going
to tell me things, huh? Oh you didn't know that didn't
you?

(CHRISTOPHER is silent.)

WARD: Take the money boy.
That's more money than you'll see in a long time.
So take the money.
What do you say?

CHRISTOPHER: Widow Luckey's…
She's expecting me for work.

WARD: Do you have any concept of what three
hundred dollars looks like in your hands?

Do you even know what three hundred dollars feels
like in your dirt-covered field-worker hands?
I'm talking about hard cash.
Three hundred dollars beautiful American currency…
Take it. Take it now…

(CHRISTOPHER *takes the envelope.*)

WARD: There…now, that's a good boy.

(CHRISTOPHER *holds the money and throws it to* WARD's
feet.)

CHRISTOPHER: I'm a man and I'm not about to be bribed
or sold off…
I don't want nothing from you.
Not now…not ever…

WARD: You're way out of your depths on this one boy.
Believe me…

(*The site of the Berry Hotel.*)

CHRISTOPHER: Evening Edwin.

EDWIN: Christopher, there's my boy.
I was just looking for you. Walk with me. Talk with
me…

CHRISTOPHER: I'd like that.

EDWIN: Boy, you know…
I got more property and money than most of these
white people in this town, not once have they added
Mister to the top of my name…
Not once…

CHRISTOPHER: Edwin, have you been drinking?

EDWIN: Yup.

CHRISTOPHER: Why?

EDWIN: Why the hell not.
You know the funny thing is, I'm going to go my grave

And people are going to believe, I ain't never touched a
drink a day in my life…You know why?
Cause I keep my life and my business separate.
Smart people do that… Are you smart Stranger?

CHRISTOPHER: Martha's going to be waiting for you.

EDWIN: Martha?

CHRISTOPHER: Your wife.

EDWIN: She's at the Opera House in Nelsonville,
watching a play…
Distance, my boy, makes marriage prosper,
Further she is away…
The less you feel you're being dragged to your death
when you see her.
Remember I said that…
God, what a disappointment I must seem to that
woman.
You know yesterday she told me,
I should never shave this mustache.
Makes me look more prestigious.
Like I'm a true businessman, she says.
I'd do everything I can to make that woman happy.

CHRISTOPHER: Let's get you home.

EDWIN: Boy, take your damn hands off me.
Can't you see you're draggin' me down?
This is my life's work.
My life.

CHRISTOPHER: I'm going home.

EDWIN: Stay damnit… You even mention the loan to
that woman, huh?

CHRISTOPHER: I did?
It didn't feel right, using her like that.

EDWIN: But using that white woman in other ways did huh?

CHRISTOPHER: That's the liquor talkin'—

EDWIN: How many more times?
How many times do I got to bend and beg for them to acknowledge me?
But I can't do it if you're busy,
Tarnishin' my name along with yours.
You're no good for people, boy, everyone around you...
I mean Jesus...Jesus... Just trouble, boy.

People are talking Stranger, don't you get that?

CHRISTOPHER: Well they ain't got nothing to talk about.

EDWIN: They don't have nothing to talk about?

CHRISTOPHER: No...

EDWIN: So people haven't seen you walkin' side by side with her? Weren't seen carrying her bags from the grocer up on Court Street, huh? Weren't chattin' up a storm with her?

CHRISTOPHER: I don't walk side by side with her.

EDWIN: So you tellin' me they haven't seen you castin' smiles in her direction?

CHRISTOPHER: I wasn't smilin' at that woman.
It was a beautiful day. I was happy that's all—

EDWIN: You're pacing—

CHRISTOPHER: That don't mean nothing.

(Silence)

EDWIN: I saw you, boy...

CHRISTOPHER: What?

EDWIN: I saw you Stranger...Saw you in that woman's arms.

CHRISTOPHER: Edwin—

EDWIN: Don't cross me boy.
You have no idea what I'm capable of.
No idea…I told you, get close…
I didn't say nothing about getting <u>that close</u>.
You're going force my hand…
Force me to sign my soul over to the devil himself, boy.
Do you realize that?

CHRISTOPHER: You got to help me.

EDWIN: Why I got to help you?

CHRISTOPHER: Cause you got me the job.

EDWIN: Well you got yourself in this damn mess.

CHRISTOPHER: Edwin—

EDWIN: For now, go home to your wife and be good to her.

CHRISTOPHER: What do I if if…
But what do I do if when I tell her… She leaves me?
What if she don't take me back?

EDWIN: Simple, way to solve that…
You don't tell her.

CHRISTOPHER: I can't do that.
I got to make things right with her.

EDWIN: Hell, I wouldn't tell my wife.
Come back home one day, find your shit outside on fire.
With her dancing around it.
Oh, you know you're in real trouble when they quiet.
Nothing scarier than a woman whose silent.
The most deadliest of storms are those that start calm and quiet…
Women aren't right, like men…
They don't take bad news well—

CHRISTOPHER: I got to tell her.

EDWIN: You love her?

CHRISTOPHER: You know I do—

EDWIN: Well let me tell you this then,
And you remember this…
I'm telling you this out of love, my boy…
Always been out of love.
Nobody is perfect in this life.
We've all sinned and sinned-alike…
Just keep that in mind.
Cause any woman that can't love you unconditionally,
Even when your man enough to admit your wrong…
You're better off alone… Cause they ain't the one for
you.

(CHRISTOPHER's home.)

CHRISTOPHER: Hey love.

NADIA: Hey—

CHRISTOPHER: Sorry I'm late…
I was over with Edwin.
Have you seen my tools…
They've gone missin'.

NADIA: Haven't seen them.
I'm about to go out in a few.

CHRISTOPHER: Any coffee on the stove?

NADIA: We're out.

CHRISTOPHER: You're mad at me?
Did I do something wrong?

NADIA: I don't know… Have you?

CHRISTOPHER: If this is about the leak on the roof.
I'll get on it tomorrow.
I made a promise but I can work on that later.

NADIA: It's mended—

CHRISTOPHER: Who fixed the roof?

NADIA: I fixed it—

CHRISTOPHER: I'm sorry…
Workin' over at Lucinda's—

NADIA: What is it you see in that woman that you don't see in me?

CHRISTOPHER: Nadia—

NADIA: I just want to understand…

CHRISTOPHER: Promise from this day forward,
I'm going to be around more.

NADIA: You promise…

CHRISTOPHER: I promise—

NADIA: Why are you opening your eyes now?

CHRISTOPHER: I finally see what I'm truly suppose to see.
You…
You're the only one who sees me
You see me for who I am, and who I can be…
I realize what I got to sacrifice…

(CHRISTOPHER *embraces* NADIA.)

(NADIA *pulls away…*)

(NADIA *struggles to breathe.*)

(*She exhales sorrow.*)

(*She's silent.*)

NADIA: How could I have been so blind?

CHRISTOPHER: If you'll just let me explain—

NADIA: What could you possibly have to explain?
All those nights I waited up for you.
All those nights I gave all my love to you…

Do you know what it's like hearing rumors.
Rumors you're laying with some widow...some old
white woman.
(*Silence*)
I'm going to ask you a question...
And I want you to answer it.
Am I right to envy this woman?
Tell me that...
(*Silence*)
I see...
(*She rises to her feet and moves to exit. A basket is in her
hand.*)

CHRISTOPHER: It was a mistake...
I don't need or want to be tangled up with that woman,
I want you—

NADIA: I see—

CHRISTOPHER: Just tell me what you want me to do and
I'll do it.
Just tell me what I got to do to make things right—

NADIA: Find new work...Come home to me...
Be a husband to me—

CHRISTOPHER: It's done...
I'm going to make things right...
I promise you that.
I'll end it anyway I got to.
I want you Nadia...I need you—

NADIA: I wish I could believe that.
(*She picks up the basket turns to leave.*)

CHRISTOPHER: What are you doing?

NADIA: Same thing I've always done...
Clean up for others.
(*She exits...*)

CHRISTOPHER: So I went to end it…

(Leaving CHRISTOPHER *standing alone. Jail cell)*

WARD: And that's when you went to Widow Luckey's and attacked her.

CHRISTOPHER: Why would I do that?

*(*LUCINDA *appears she's plucking the petals of a white flower.)*

WARD: Maybe you started feeling things,
Were starting to feel strangled by the situation. Maybe?
Lust can cause a man's heart to grow hard…
Maybe you broke into her place for money,
Since that loan Edwin wanted didn't come through…
Since she was there you couldn't help,
But want to get yourself a taste—

CHRISTOPHER: When Widow Luckey wakes up she can tell you the truth—

LUCINDA: He loves me…

WARD: Lucinda not going to wake up.

CHRISTOPHER: What?

WARD: She's gone.

LUCINDA: He loves me not…

CHRISTOPHER: What do you mean?

WARD: She's at peace. She's dead. You killed her.
(Pause)
No, matter Edwin will tell me everything I need to know.

CHRISTOPHER: Edwin?

WARD: Yes, maybe he'll help get to the root of all this.
(To EDWIN*)*
Talk some sense into this boy,

Convince your colleague here; that signing the confession is in his best interest.

EDWIN: How is he?

WARD: Better than he would be out there.

EDWIN: May I speak to Christopher, in private for a moment, sir.

WARD: Go on ahead.
(He takes a few steps back but doesn't leave.)

EDWIN: They treatin' you alright?
(Silence)
This is a terrible thing that's happened here, boy.
Slippery slope, very slippery slope indeed.

CHRISTOPHER: Edwin, you got to help me.
You got to tell him I'm innocent.
Tell him I didn't do the crime, Edwin.
Tell him he's got the wrong man, Edwin.
They'll listen to you Edwin.
Tell him he got to let me go.

EDWIN: Damnit, will you hush, boy.
What you doin' lettin' these white folks seein' they got you scared?
Calm yourself.
(Silence)
Good…
Now you know, I always look out for you boy.

CHRISTOPHER: I know.

EDWIN: And you know I only want what's best for you, right?

CHRISTOPHER: Yeah, Edwin, I know.

EDWIN: Don't you understand what's happening here?
You're in a bad spot, a real bad spot.
Can't you see this is bad for not just you,

This is bad for me, for Nadia, for this town,
Everyone around you.

CHRISTOPHER: I understand that but—

EDWIN: Do you? Do you really?
Ward ain't a bad man,
He's trying to help you.
Sheriff could just hand you over to those white folks
out there.
Let them have their way with you.
But he's not. He's not.
He's trying to help you.
He's offering you the chance to tell your side of things
to a jury, to get you a fair trial.

CHRISTOPHER: Fair trial?
We both know I wouldn't get no fair trial.

EDWIN: You don't know that for sure.

CHRISTOPHER: I didn't do this.

EDWIN: You think those white folk out there care?
You think they give a damn about you, boy?
To them you ain't nothin' but a colored boy they
wanna see hang.
Now hear me out, boy.
You got to sign that confession.
Sign it…sign it…so you can walk this earth one more
day
That's all we trying to do.
Save you.
So, what you waitin' for, take that man's offer and sign
it.
Innocent, guilty, it don't matter.
Sign that confession so that mob will be appeased.

WARD: Time is ticking down, gentlemen.

CHRISTOPHER: Edwin.

EDWIN: Christopher, listen to me to my damnit,
You found yourself in the worst kinda situation a man
can get himself into.
You're a good man.
A kind, good hearted man.
I just want what's best for you.

CHRISTOPHER: But I didn't do it?
I wouldn't hurt Widow Luckey.

EDWIN: You know that for sure?

CHRISTOPHER: What you mean?

EDWIN: Everybody around here know you got those
visions.
But my question is…
When those visions come, where your mind go?
Can you honestly say you got full control of yourself?
Can you account for everything that happens in those
moments?
I've seen you when you have them…
You there but at the same time not.
It's a frightening sight to see.
So can you honestly say you couldn't have attacked
her?

CHRISTOPHER: I wouldn't attack her.

EDWIN: Can you honestly say you got full control of
yourself, Christopher?

CHRISTOPHER: I don't know—

EDWIN: That's the phrase right there.
You don't know…
Let me tell you what the sheriff got on you.
A busted down door, your employer layin' dead in her
own blood, and your bloody hatchet buried in her, you

with no claims of where you was, and a town scared of you cause of them visions.

You understand what I'm sayin, boy?

CHRISTOPHER: But I didn't kill her.

EDWIN: Can you say that for sure?
Can you say that for sure Christopher?

CHRISTOPHER: What would you do?

EDWIN: I'm not you, Stranger.

CHRISTOPHER: But what would you do?
What would you do if you were me?

EDWIN: Me? I like getting to wake up in the morning.
Stretching, yawning, seeing the sunrise peak over the treeline to greet me one more day.
I know it's not much but that's where I find my joy.
Starts me off right, knowing I'm alive to see a new day.
So what I'd do, is I'd say my prayers.
Get right with the Lord
Then I'd take a deep breath. I'd ask for that man's pen.
Take that paper he's got there and I'd sign my name on the line.
And then I'd know that I'm going to live just a few more nights.
See a few more sunrises.
That's what I'd do.
That knowledge alone would be the world to me.

CHRISTOPHER: I can't do that.

EDWIN: Yes, you can boy,
So that mob don't burn your feet, gorge out your eyes, beat you near to death, and then wait til you beg for death before they finally hang you from the nearest bridge or tree they can find.
Yes, you can.

So Nadia, don't have to suffer knowing you died a
horrible death.
Yes you can. Yes you can. Yes you can, boy.
Yes you will.
Cause I love you too damn much boy to see you die
that way.
You'll go to trial.
I'll hire on a good lawyer for you.
Get Mr. Loevner to represent you.
Best in town.
But first you do what needs to be done, sign that
confession.

CHRISTOPHER: Edwin, I can't…

EDWIN: You must!!!
(Silence)
You think on it.
All I want you to do right now is think on it, boy.
(He walks away towards WARD.*)*

*(*CHRISTOPHER *sits.)*

EDWIN: Just give him a few to stew on my words.
The boy will realize what's good for him and sign,
Mark my words, sheriff, he'll do it.
Now my compass led me in the direction, you pointed
me, sir.
This along with what else you requested is sitting on
your deputy's desk,
If memory serves me correct you promised for my civic
duty, something in return.
(Silence)

WARD: I did indeed.

*(*WARD *holds out towards* EDWIN *a small envelope. Almost
hands it over and stops.)*

*(*LUCINDA *appears plucking petals from a white flower.)*

LUCINDA: He loves me.

(WARD *hands* EDWIN *the signed loan.*)

WARD: Congrats Mr Berry, I'm going to enjoy our future business endeavor together.

EDWIN: Could you perhaps say that one more time for me, sheriff.
Just that first part.

LUCINDA: He loves me not.

WARD: Congrats. Mister. Berry.

EDWIN: I must admit I do like how that sounds.

WARD: Well I must say I appreciate you coming down and helping to do the right thing.

LUCINDA: He loves me.

EDWIN: There's no such thing as right and wrong, sheriff,
It's about business, always been about business.

(CHRISTOPHER *takes a deep breath as he overhears.*)

CHRISTOPHER: One brick at a time Edwin, one brick at a time.

LUCINDA: He loves me not.

(*Evening*…CHRISTOPHER *and* LUCINDA)

LUCINDA: Hello come in…
(*Pause*)
Everything alright?

CHRISTOPHER: I'm fine.

LUCINDA: Storm is going to be approachin' soon.
I can feel it in my bones…I'm looking forward to it.

CHRISTOPHER: I'm not.

(*Silence*)

LUCINDA: I couldn't sleep last night…

I took a walk along the river though…
Picked white daisies.
I probably look a complete mess right now.

CHRISTOPHER: I like your hair that way.

LUCINDA: What?
Down like this?

CHRISTOPHER: You should wear it like that more often.

LUCINDA: Me…I'm an old woman, It's not—

CHRISTOPHER / LUCINDA: Proper—

LUCINDA: I can't be havin' the whole town,
look at me like I'm some kinda hussy.
Can you picture that, you and me arm in arm…
Entangled in lovers' embraces like nothing else matters
Walking Court Street with my hair down?
Like this?
No… Certainly not proper.
Time after time we keep coming back to that word.

CHRISTOPHER: Perhaps you're right.
Then again I'll never get to walk down Court Street…
With you.

CHRISTOPHER / LUCINDA: I want to talk to you about
something.

CHRISTOPHER: You first…

(LUCINDA *pulls out a small box.*)

LUCINDA: It's not made in China,
Or tailored by the finest in New York, or London.
But Mr Wagner is said to be the best tailor in Athens.
I hope you like it.

CHRISTOPHER: What's this?

LUCINDA: Open it and see.
Well, come on now…

Open it.

(CHRISTOPHER *opens it and pulls out a red waistcoat.*)

LUCINDA: It's not made of velvet, but still elegant in fashion and style.
A tree is woven into the designed on the back of it.
Twisted like the scars on Christopher's back.

CHRISTOPHER: Lucinda.

LUCINDA: I know you think those scars upon your back are…ugly…
But I wanted to show you through this design woven into the back of this, how beautiful they truly are to look upon.

CHRISTOPHER: You just don't get it.

LUCINDA: I want you to see the beauty you possess.
Take it. Don't say a word, just take it please—

(*Silence*)

CHRISTOPHER: This isn't right. This isn't right. This isn't right.

LUCINDA: Please…
Just…
Look what else is in the box.

(CHRISTOPHER *reaches into the box and pulls out a ticket.*)

(*Silence*)

LUCINDA: We should leave this place… You and I…
Together.

CHRISTOPHER: And go where?

LUCINDA: Anywhere but this Valley.

CHRISTOPHER: Where we going to go?
You think it's as easy as that?

LUCINDA: I could pull out all my money,
And we could…

We could take the first boat to Europe.

CHRISTOPHER: You'd leave your entire life behind?

LUCINDA: I've never felt more alive in my fifty some
odd years of life…
Than in these last weeks…Than in these last hours…
Run away with me…
We could go to Europe… See the greater world.
Christopher you should forget about investing in some
silly hotel.
I mean a hotel here really? And you won't need to
worry about Nadia…

CHRISTOPHER: Stop it.

LUCINDA: We could leave her some money,
Make sure she's well taken care of… She'd want for
nothing.

CHRISTOPHER: Leave her out of this.

LUCINDA: I'm simply saying she can't make you happy.
Not like I can.

(CHRISTOPHER *grabs a hold of* LUCINDA. *Grips her tight.*)

CHRISTOPHER: And I said leave her out of this.

LUCINDA: Christopher please you're hurting me.

(CHRISTOPHER *releases* LUCINDA, *pushing her away.*)

(CHRISTOPHER *stares out into the distance.*)

CHRISTOPHER: I'm sorry.

LUCINDA: I don't understand…
I don't understand why you're acting like this.

CHRISTOPHER: I can't do this…

LUCINDA: Come away with me…
Here you'll always be seen as less than you are.
I'm giving you a chance.

CHRISTOPHER: Think about what you're saying.

LUCINDA: It doesn't have to be this way…
I read in a magazine…

CHRISTOPHER: To hell with your magazines, Lucinda—

LUCINDA: I've frightened you with my talk.
Can't you sit with me for awhile, before you have to go?
I can cook something. Do you want something to drink?

CHRISTOPHER: I'm fine.

LUCINDA: It's been awhile since I've felt a touch from someone.
You know that?
Had somebody look at me like you do…
For the first time in a long time…
I didn't have someone looking at me,
Like I was a wife, a mother, a widow…
You looked at me with those eyes and…
Looked at me, for once like I was a woman.
I want to thank you for that.

CHRISTOPHER: You don't gotta thank me.

LUCINDA: No but I do…

CHRISTOPHER: I can't do this…Don't this feel wrong to you?

LUCINDA: What?

CHRISTOPHER: Don't you feel any guilt in that soul of yours?

LUCINDA: Should I?

CHRISTOPHER: Lucinda—

LUCINDA: No, you tell me?

CHRISTOPHER: For what will be three, coming on four weeks now.

I make my way down here every morning.
I work, I tend to the things that need tending to.
And then I lay with you, tend to your needs.
But I can't do it any more.

LUCINDA: Christopher...

CHRISTOPHER: I'm a married man...
At first I thought that guilt in me would go away.
Each time I think it will be easier than the next.
But it don't...I still have that feeling inside of me.
Making it hard for me to breath around her,
Around you...I'm choking myself...
I can't do this any more...

LUCINDA: I thought we shared something—

CHRISTOPHER: We do...
We did—

LUCINDA: Why are you doing this?

CHRISTOPHER: I owed that woman I married the truth—

LUCINDA: We write our own truth.
Christopher...wait, I want you to have the waistcoat.

CHRISTOPHER: I don't know if I could do that...ma'am.

(*Silence. It's long and cold.*)

LUCINDA: Please...I want you to have it.
It would mean a lot to me.

(CHRISTOPHER *takes the waistcoat.*)

LUCINDA: Put it on for me.
I want to see you in it.

(CHRISTOPHER *hesitates and places the waistcoat on.*)

LUCINDA: Well mercy on my soul you look quite charming,
If I do say so myself.
If I didn't know any better...

I might mistake you for a fine business man
Now, I just want you to do me favor,
Will you do that for me?

CHRISTOPHER: What?

LUCINDA: I need you to consider this closely for me.
When you're at home with you're her.
When you sit down to dinner with her,
When you lay in bed next to her…
When your loving her and growing old with her.
I want you to consider how good of a life you could
have had…
With me.
Please will you do that for me?
Just put the ticket in your pocket and think on it.
I'm getting on that train tomorrow night,
And on the boat to Europe shortly afterwards…come
with me.
You decide to stay I'll sign for the loan, but come see
me.

CHRISTOPHER: I got to go back to her.
I thought I could be a lover to you and a husband to
her…
But I can't…I can't be both.

(LUCINDA *kisses* CHRISTOPHER *on the cheek and tucks one
of the tickets into his waistcoat. She shows him the other and
places it into her apron.*)

LUCINDA: I'm certain that when the time comes,
You'll make the right decision…

(CHRISTOPHER *exits and sits in his cell.*)

LUCINDA: I love you…

(NADIA *enters.*)

WARD: Nadia, you shouldn't be here?

NADIA: Sheriff, you mind if I speak with my husband for a moment?

WARD: Of course…of course…

(Pause)

NADIA: Are you alright in here?

CHRISTOPHER: I wish you hadn't of come—

NADIA: Well, I did…

(Silence. CHRISTOPHER and NADIA look at each other for a long time. They really see who each other is.)

CHRISTOPHER: How many out there?

NADIA: It's growin'.

CHRISTOPHER: I don't want you to see me like this.
(He takes her hand and kisses each fingers. One by one)
I love you Nadia…
(He embraces her tightly.)

(CHRISTOPHER looks at NADIA. She looks at him.)

(She slaps him.)

NADIA: I want you to know…
I can't love you anymore.
It hurts too much…
I feel like our love is choking me
and I can't do that to myself.
Knowing I'm carrying your child.

CHRISTOPHER: What?

NADIA: Three months with child, Stranger…
Three months with child…three months and you couldn't see.

CHRISTOPHER: Why didn't you tell me?

NADIA: Why couldn't you see it!!!
Tell me that, Christopher.

Why couldn't you see it?
You could see inside of everybody else, but you
couldn't see me!
You couldn't see inside of me!
(Pause)
I wanted to tell you so badly,
But you only saw and heard what you wanted to.
So consumed by your dreams and your nightmares…
I wondered when you'd open your eyes…
See why I needed you and you couldn't do that.
What am I suppose to do with a man like that?

CHRISTOPHER: I don't know…Nadia—

NADIA: God, I thought you were such a good man.
Saw you for so much more than just a man.
You were blessed. You were everything. But you're
not… You're…
(She pulls out the ticket.)
I've got to leave you,
I'm leaving the Valley,
There's nothing here for me in Athens no more.
You destroyed everything good I had here, everything.
(She kisses him upon the cheek and she turns to leave.)

CHRISTOPHER: And with a single kiss upon the cheek,
Judas betrayed Jaysus.
I could never see into you.
(Silence)
No matter how hard I tried, I just couldn't do it.
And I'm sorry for that…I'm sorry I couldn't see till
now.

NADIA: Judas? I'm the Judas?!!
Do you see how you hurt me…
Do you see how you hurt our child…
Hurt us…

Can you see that?

CHRISTOPHER: I see…I can see…

(NADIA *rises to her feet and turns to exit facing* WARD.)

NADIA: Sheriff, you seem to have made a mistake.

WARD: How's that?

NADIA: You brought me to see my husband.
But this man right here ain't nuthin' but a stranger to me.

(She exits.)

(CHRISTOPHER *cries violent tears…*)

(Dry pain filled sobs and as quickly as the tears began to flow. They stop replaced by a soft mournful humming. WARD *approaches.)*

CHRISTOPHER: You mind if I take a sip from that flask.

WARD: Thought you didn't drink.

CHRISTOPHER: Same here.

He drinks.

WARD: You ready to sign?

CHRISTOPHER: I'm ready…
(He takes the confession.)
(He takes a pen and holds it to the paper. He signs it. Folds it carefully)
Sheriff, I once told my wife I'd die if I ever hurt her.

WARD: I'm sorry, It's got to be this way, son.
Now I got to go out there and show that confession to those men outside. Convince them that justice has been done, and they can go home to their families before they do something that'll forever haunt their souls.
This will buy us some time.

I'm not much of a religious man, but I've always
believed the most precious gift God ever gave man was
life…
I like to think he's right, about that.

(CHRISTOPHER *laughs*.)

WARD:What's so funny?

CHRISTOPHER: No, you're wrong. It was love.
(*He stops, looks at* WARD *before ripping the confession*.)
Sheriff, You go out to the mob gathering out there…
Let them know I can't wait for them to see me.

(*End scene*)

Epilogue

(CHRISTOPHER *stands there half naked, upon the stump*.)

(LUCINDA *and* NADIA *appear*.)

(*A basket is in* NADIA's *hand*.)

CHRISTOPHER: It's strange what comes to your mind
when you're about to die. How everything starts
becoming clearer.

LUCINDA: May I help you?

NADIA: Yes, ma'am… You can.

CHRISTOPHER: Your thoughts don't go to the pain you
feel as the mob beats you nearly to death. You don't
concentrate on the noose wrapping around your neck,
or the angry cries for blood heard surrounding you.

LUCINDA: Well,what can I do for you?

NADIA: You know who I am, don't you?

LUCINDA: Yes, I know.

CHRISTOPHER: I thought back to that hot August
morning as a child when that old woman held my

small hand and showed me that man dangling from the tree.

And she told me, "Don't you ever forget what love will bring you."

(He begins wrapping and tangling the ropes around himself.)

It was at that moment it all made sense to me.

LUCINDA: You're beautiful, I see why Christopher loves you.

NADIA: May I talk to you?

CHRISTOPHER: Love is like an old tree,
twisted and tangled upon itself from time.

NADIA: Can I be honest with you, Ma'am?

LUCINDA: Yes please do.

CHRISTOPHER: Roots buried deep into the depth of the earth.

NADIA: I envy you... No, not envy...I hate you...

(LUCINDA steps back.)

CHRISTOPHER: Choking on its own angry weeds unable to grow straight and produce fruit out of fear of its own damn self.

NADIA: I had a good life, a happy life.
It may not have been a great life...But it was good.

CHRISTOPHER: The leaves that once produced shade are no longer refreshing to savor is now a cold lonely shadow you got to live every waking torturous moment underneath...

NADIA: Now lately, I've tried as I made this walk over here...
Tried to understand what went wrong...

CHRISTOPHER: And you find yourself out of disgust and shame wanting to wrap these wicked vines around your own neck…

NADIA: Why my husband would feel a need to lay down with you.
And I don't see it…

CHRISTOPHER: Cause you know you need to hang for the crime you committed…
Of breaking the heart of the woman that you love…

NADIA: I'm trying to understand what he sees in you… Why he would do something like this, what he sees in you that he doesn't in me…I don't see it…

CHRISTOPHER: And worst yet…
(He reaches out towards NADIA.)

LUCINDA: What have you got in that basket?

(NADIA opens the basket and pulls out a hatchet.)

NADIA: I want you to show me what he sees inside of you.

CHRISTOPHER: You face a fate far worse than death…

NADIA: Can you show me?

CHRISTOPHER: An empty soul.

(Lights out on LUCINDA and NADIA leaving CHRISTOPHER alone in darkness.)

(CHRISTOPHER stands wrapped in his ropes.)

(A twisted tree tangled and choking upon its own vines.)

(Black out)

END OF PLAY

www.ingramcontent.com/pod-product-compliance
Lightning Source LLC
Chambersburg PA
CBHW052137090426
42741CB00009B/2116